A Taste of Herbs

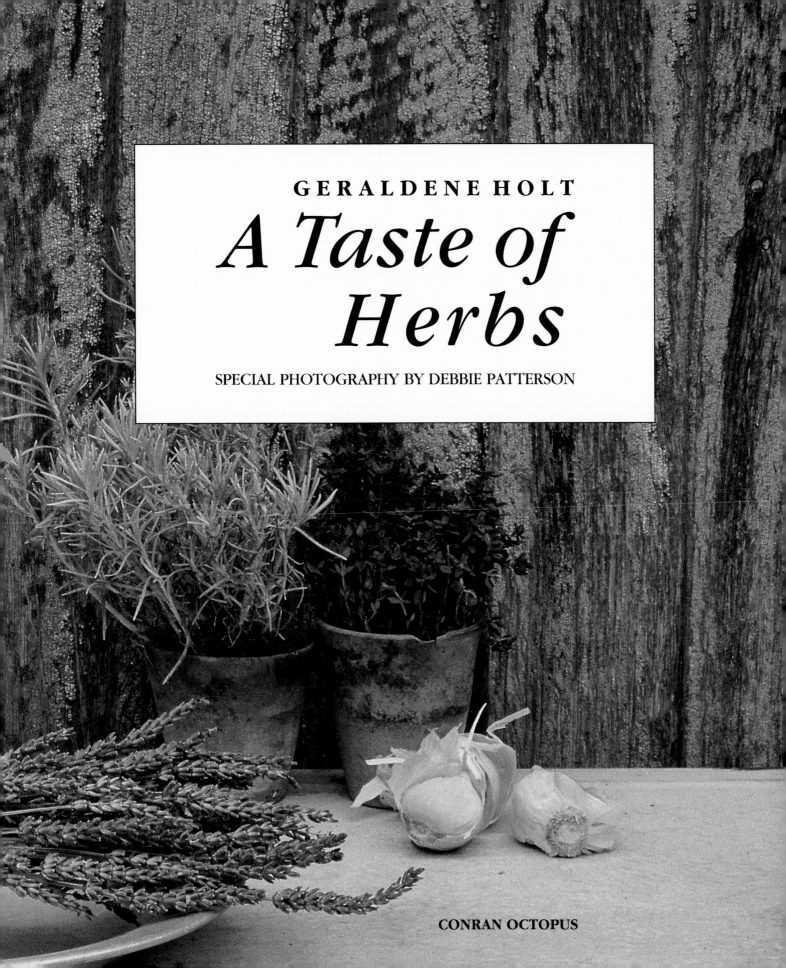

GERALDENE HOLT

A Taste of
Herbs

SPECIAL PHOTOGRAPHY BY DEBBIE PATTERSON

CONRAN OCTOPUS

First published in 1993 by
Conran Octopus Limited
37 Shelton Street
London WC2H 9HN

This volume was originally published as one section of
Geraldene Holt's Complete Book of Herbs in 1991 by
Conran Octopus Limited

PROJECT EDITOR **JOANNA COPESTICK**
EDITOR **NORMA MACMILLAN**
EDITORIAL ASSISTANT **ROD MACKENZIE**
ART EDITOR **KAREN BOWEN**
PICTURE RESEARCH **JESSICA WALTON**
PRODUCTION **JULIA GOLDING**
HOME ECONOMIST **JANE SUTHERING**
ASSISTED BY **MEG JANSZ**
SPECIAL PHOTOGRAPHY **DEBBIE PATTERSON**

A CIP catalogue record for this book is available from the
British Library

ISBN 1 85029 500 X

Printed and bound in Singapore
Typeset by Servis Filmsetting Limited
Colour separation by Chroma Graphics (Overseas) Pty
Limited

CONTENTS

INTRODUCTION

*Good living is an act of intelligence, by which we
choose things which have an agreeable taste
rather than those which do not.*
BRILLAT-SAVARIN, 'THE PHYSIOLOGY OF TASTE', 1826

To my mind it has always seemed simply intelligent to eat, and, if possible, to cultivate those plants which prosper in our own climate and to develop ways of preparing them which enhance their intrinsic good flavour. In all probability, no plant rewards the cook as agreeably as a fine herb.

The fortunes of these historic plants that have changed little in the course of time, have remained constant despite the ebb and flow of fashion in food, medicine and gardening. Few plants have survived so faithfully, for the hybridizer has rarely introduced new varieties. Indeed, left to their own devices some herbs such as mint hybridize themselves.

Some ways of cooking with herbs have also survived from ancient times. Consider the fondness for garlic which characterized the food of ancient Rome, and its present-day place in Californian cuisine. Or reflect on the role played by herbs such as sweet bay, tarragon and parsley in French cooking today – both bourgeois and haute cuisine. It is as vital as ever. This allegiance to particular plants has happened because the taste of herbs is too good to miss. And once adopted is never abandoned.

The versatility of herbs has never been in doubt. It seems extraordinary that a small sprig of fresh rosemary can embody so many valuable properties. In cooking, rosemary transfers its flavour to a dish and subtly transforms and elevates its taste. As, for instance, when a roast leg of lamb, imbued with the pervasive and haunting flavour of the herb, becomes a more complete dish requiring no embellishment. The rosemary, in effect, rounds out and amplifies the flavour of the meat and makes it taste more satisfying and pleasing to the discriminating palate. Yet when the same herb perfumes an ice-cream or a plate of warm, buttery biscuits a discreetly altered, more delicate scent is produced because the essential oils in the herb have reacted with different ingredients in the food.

The practised cook soon learns that herbs are an ingredient to be trusted – fresh herbs are pure, unspoilt and essential. No sensible cook would want to ignore herbs or banish them from his cooking. For the capacity of these generous and beguiling plants to transform our food, engage our senses and delight our palate appears infinite.

*Asparagus with Lemon and Tarragon Mousseline
Sauce – a delicious springtime taste of herbs.*
See the recipe for this dish on page 56.

SOUPS AND FIRST COURSES

There's no doubt that first impressions matter, gastronomically speaking, however
one might wish to deny it. The table is laid, the plate is placed before you
and, full of expectation, you respond to the appearance and aroma of the dish.
The first course is an introduction or overture to any meal and as such it should
impart an obvious, appetizing appeal that says 'eat-me'.
Fortunately, most good food prepared with fresh seasonal ingredients to an
appropriate recipe does look attractive: it should not require any additional tweaking
on the plate. Learning how to trap the elusive scent of a herb in one's cooking takes time.
There are some useful guidelines though. It is usually helpful to know the native
habitat of culinary herbs. For example, rosemary is a Mediterranean herb
that grows wild on the hillsides of Provence. The herb is widely used
in the cooking of the region, most notably in the slowly cooked daubes of pork and beef.
From this starting point it is interesting to discover how well a sprig of rosemary
enhances other casseroled dishes, such as a chicken or beef stew.
So why not add the herb to a beef stock and use it in a soup?
Some of my recipes for cooking with herbs – for instance, the Tomato Tarts
(see page 19) – start with a nod to these well-established culinary alliances.
Others, like the Courgette and Sorrel Soup (see page 18), were inspired by my garden,
where the two principal ingredients grow alongside each other and reach a peak
of perfection at the same time. I hope that you will find all of them
not only delicious but also a starting point for your own culinary adventures.

PREVIOUS PAGE *left to right* SCALLOPS WITH ROASTED PEPPERS AND MINT IN A FILO BASKET, *page 13*;
PUMPKIN AND ROSEMARY SOUP WITH SUN-DRIED TOMATO CROÛTES, *page 13*;
CHILLED AVOCADO AND BASIL SOUP WITH ASPARAGUS CRACKERS, *page 14*.

SCALLOPS WITH ROASTED PEPPERS AND MINT IN A FILO BASKET

This dish has become one of my favourite starts to a summer meal. Use fresh plump scallops for the best flavour, or replace the scallops with small slices of monkfish. The filo pastry baskets can be made well ahead of time and frozen until needed.

SERVES 4
6 shelled scallops with their corals
juice of 1 lemon
1 red sweet pepper
4–8 sheets of filo pastry
30g (1oz) butter, melted
salt
6 pink peppercorns, crushed
2 tablespoons extra virgin olive oil
a sliver of garlic, chopped
2 teaspoons chopped mint
4 sprigs of mint, to garnish

Use kitchen paper to pat the scallops dry and, if necessary, remove the fine black thread from each one. Detach the corals and then cut each scallop into three slices. Put the scallops and corals on a plate and sprinkle with a little lemon juice. Set aside in a cool place.

Roast the red pepper on a heatproof plate under a grill set on high, turning the pepper over until the skin is blistered and even blackened in places. Remove from the heat, cover with an upturned bowl and leave for 15 minutes (this makes the pepper easier to peel). Skin the pepper, cut it in half and remove the core and seeds, then cut the flesh into narrow strips. Set aside.

Spread a sheet of filo pastry on the work surface and brush it with butter. Cut the pastry in half and place one piece in a buttered bun tin, gently pressing the pastry into shape. Allow the surplus pastry to spread out from the tin like a handkerchief. Place the second piece of pastry on top of the first but slightly twisted round so that the pastry corners do not overlap. Slightly crinkle the edges of the pastry to make a basket shape. Make the other pastry cases in the same way.

Bake in a moderately hot oven (200°C, 400°F, gas mark 6) for 5–8 minutes until the pastry is golden and crisp. Cool in the tin for 2 minutes, then transfer to four individual plates and keep warm.

Season the scallops with salt and pink peppercorns. Heat the olive oil with the garlic in a frying pan and cook the slices of scallop briefly on each side. Add the corals and the mint and cook for 1 minute, then use a slotted spoon to transfer the fish to a hot plate. Add the roasted peppers to the pan and heat.

Spoon the peppers and the scallops into the pastry baskets. Add some lemon juice to the the pan and when bubbling, pour over the scallops. Garnish each basket with mint.

GARDEN HERB SORBET

The inspiration for this lovely sorbet came from Alan Ford, the talented chef at Hintlesham Hall, a magnificent Elizabethan country house in Suffolk with a beautiful herb garden.

SERVES 6–8
150ml ($\frac{1}{4}$ pint) medium dry white wine
700ml (1$\frac{1}{4}$ pints) water
225g (8oz) sugar
$\frac{1}{2}$ cinnamon stick
6 cloves
a large handful of 3 freshly picked garden herbs e.g. mint, parsley and basil
2 teaspoons finely chopped garden herbs
sprigs of mint, parsley or basil, to decorate

Measure the wine and water into a saucepan, add the sugar and stir over low heat until dissolved. Add the cinnamon and cloves and bring to the boil. Simmer steadily for 4 minutes. Remove from the heat and add the handful of herbs. Leave to infuse for 1 hour.

Strain the syrup into a bowl and stir in the finely chopped herbs. Freeze in a sorbetière or in a freezer until firm. Half an hour before serving, beat the sorbet until it is fairly smooth and then refreeze.

To serve, scoop the sorbet into stemmed glasses and decorate with sprigs of herb.

PUMPKIN AND ROSEMARY SOUP WITH SUN-DRIED TOMATO CROUTES

It is a charming idea to serve this soup in the pumpkin shell itself – it makes a natural tureen and even has its own lid.

SERVES 6
60g (2oz) butter
2 shallots, finely chopped
900g (2lb) pumpkin flesh, diced
a sprig of fresh rosemary
5cm (2in) stick of cinnamon
1 litre (1$\frac{3}{4}$ pints) chicken stock
150ml ($\frac{1}{4}$ pint) double cream
salt and freshly milled pepper
SUN-DRIED TOMATO CROUTES
2 sun-dried tomatoes
4 tablespoons hot water
1 slim clove garlic, chopped
120g (4oz) butter
a squeeze of lemon juice
1 French loaf, sliced

Melt the butter in a saucepan and stir in the shallots. Cook over medium heat for 5–8 minutes until soft, but do not allow the shallots to brown. Stir in the pumpkin until coated in butter. Add the sprig of rosemary and the cinnamon, cover the pan and cook over medium heat for 15 minutes.

Add the stock and cook, covered, for 20–30 minutes until the pumpkin is soft.

Meanwhile, prepare the croûtes. Soften the sun-dried tomatoes in the hot water. Drain and use scissors to snip the tomatoes into a food processor. Add the garlic and butter and process until the tomato is finely chopped and the butter is an attractive coral colour. Mix in the lemon juice to adjust the flavour.

Discard the sprig of rosemary and the cinnamon from the pumpkin mixture and purée the contents of the pan in a food processor. Return the soup to the pan. Add the cream, reheat and season. Keep hot until ready to serve.

Add a swirl of cream to the soup just before serving. Toast the slices of bread, spread with the tomato and garlic butter and serve.

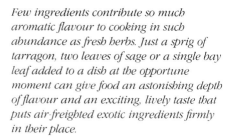

Few ingredients contribute so much aromatic flavour to cooking in such abundance as fresh herbs. Just a sprig of tarragon, two leaves of sage or a single bay leaf added to a dish at the opportune moment can give food an astonishing depth of flavour and an exciting, lively taste that puts air-freighted exotic ingredients firmly in their place.

CHILLED AVOCADO AND BASIL SOUP WITH ASPARAGUS CRACKERS

This delicious soup is best made ahead and chilled. The asparagus crackers taste at their best hot from the oven, when the filo pastry is still crisp and golden and the asparagus in basil butter is tender and juicy.

SERVES 6–7
3 large, ripe avocado pears
1 teaspoon basil leaves snipped into pieces
a sliver of garlic, crushed
a few drops of elderflower vinegar (see page 79) or balsamic vinegar
juice of ½ lemon
300ml (½ pint) Greek-style natural yoghurt
about 450ml (¾ pint) asparagus or vegetable stock
salt
leaves of basil, to garnish
ASPARAGUS CRACKERS
24 asparagus tips, each 7.5–10cm (3–4in) long
120g (4oz) butter, softened
1 teaspoon finely chopped basil or a combination of chives and thyme
a squeeze of lemon juice
8 sheets of filo pastry, each measuring 18 × 38cm (7 × 15in)

Halve the avocado pears, discard the stones and scrape the flesh into a food processor. Add the basil, garlic, vinegar, lemon juice and yoghurt and whizz together until smooth. Thin to the desired consistency with the stock, then season with salt. Pour into a jug and chill.

Trim the cut-end end of each spear of asparagus, then cook them in boiling salted water for 5–8 minutes until tender. Refresh in cold water and drain well.

Blend the butter with the basil and lemon juice, and leave in a warm place until soft.

Stack the sheets of filo pastry and divide into three by making two even cuts in the shorter direction to produce 24 pieces, each measuring 18 × 13cm (7 × 5in). Take one piece of pastry and brush the centre with basil butter; also brush basil butter over a spear of asparagus. Place the asparagus in the centre of the piece of pastry and wrap up like a Christmas cracker. Tie each end together using several 15cm (6in) lengths of blanched chive stalks. Place on a buttered baking sheet and brush the pastry with basil butter. Make the rest of the asparagus crackers.

Bake in a moderately hot oven (200°C, 400°F, gas mark 6) for 8–12 minutes until the pastry is crisp and golden.

Pour the chilled soup into a tureen or ladle into individual soup bowls. Garnish each bowl with a basil leaf and place 3–4 asparagus crackers beside each bowl.

BABY VEGETABLES WITH HERB BUTTER EN PAPILLOTE

Cooking food in a paper bag, or en papillote, *is not only fun – it also makes good sense, because all the intense delicious flavour of these baby vegetables bathed in herb butter is contained in the parcel until the moment when you tear into the paper and the aroma bursts forth.*

SERVES 4
450g (1lb) mixed baby vegetables such as baby leeks, baby sweetcorn, broccoli and cauliflower florets, carrots, courgettes, mangetout peas and baby turnips
2–3 faggots of garden herbs
salt
120g (4oz) butter, softened
2–3 tablespoons chopped mixed garden herbs
a squeeze of lemon juice

Prepare the vegetables by washing and trimming as necessary. Place the faggots of herbs in a steaming basket and arrange the vegetables on top. Steam the vegetables until almost cooked, then remove from the basket and season lightly, if desired, with salt.

Cream the butter with the chopped herbs and add lemon juice to taste. Place a sheet of baking parchment on the work surface, fold it in half and then open again. Spread some herb butter in the centre of the sheet and arrange one-quarter of the vegetables on one side of the fold line. Spoon herb butter on top of the vegetables. Fold over the paper and secure the edges by folding neatly – or fasten the paper with old-fashioned wooden clothes' pegs. Make 3 more paper parcels in the same way.

Bake the vegetable parcels on a baking tray in a moderately hot oven (200°C, 400°F, gas mark 6) for 10 minutes until the vegetables are tender. Carefully transfer the parcels to 4 individual hot plates and serve straight away.

Baby vegetables cooked en papillote *(in paper) provide sealed parcels that, when opened on the dining table, reveal a delicious and colourful herb-scented dish.*

MISTICANZA
WITH WOOD-EAR MUSHROOMS

Misticanza *is the musical name for the Italian mixture of wild leaves and herbs collected from the fields and meadows of Castelli-Romani. According to Anna Del Conte's superb* Gastronomy of Italy, *Roman gastronomes state that* misticanza *should contain 21 different kinds of wild salad. She writes, 'Even if this is a little excessive, a good* misticanza *must contain rocket, chicory, sorrel, mint, radichella – a kind of dandelion – valerianella, lamb's lettuce, purslane and other local edible weeds.' For a late summer or early autumn dish, I have combined a lightly dressed* misticanza *with warm wood-ear mushrooms (oyster mushrooms are also highly delicious served this way) cooked in hazelnut oil.*

FOR EACH SERVING
a large handful of *misticanza* leaves
a dressing made with extra virgin oil,
tarragon vinegar, salt and freshly milled
pepper
about 1 handful of wood-ear mushrooms
sunflower oil
hazelnut oil
lemon juice
a few toasted hazelnuts, sliced

If necessary, wash and dry the leaves of *misticanza* by shaking them in a salad basket.

Make the dressing in a bowl and, just before serving, gently toss the leaves in it until very lightly coated, then arrange on a plate.

Cut the wood-ear mushrooms from their stalk and dice the stalk. Gently cook the mushrooms in sunflower oil until soft, adding a little hazelnut oil towards the end of the cooking time. Season with lemon juice and salt, if desired.

Spoon the wood-ear mushrooms over the *misticanza*. Add the hazelnuts to the hot pan, add a squeeze of lemon juice and stir to incorporate all the cooking juices. Spoon the hazelnuts and cooking juices over the mushrooms and serve straight away while the mushrooms are still warm.

MALAYSIAN SPICED FISH
IN NEW LEAVES

I devised this dish a year or so ago for a New Year's Day brunch – hence the pun. The oriental combination of hot fish balls wrapped in cool herbs and leaves of lettuce is always appetizing but not too filling.

SERVES 4
225g (8oz) fresh haddock, skinned and
boned
120g (4oz) prawns, cooked and peeled
60g (2oz) shelled almonds, blanched and
chopped
30g (1oz) cooked ham, diced
a sliver of garlic, chopped
a walnut-size piece of fresh root ginger,
peeled and grated
1 tablespoon safflower oil
1 teaspoon cornflour
$\frac{1}{4}$ teaspoon salt
1 teaspoon soy sauce
oil for shallow frying
SAUCE
1 teaspoon light sesame oil
1 teaspoon light soy sauce
1 teaspoon white wine vinegar
$\frac{1}{2}$ teaspoon clear honey
$\frac{1}{4}$ fresh green or red chilli, chopped
a sliver of garlic
2 tablespoons hot water
TO SERVE
1 small iceberg lettuce
leaves of mint
leaves of coriander

First make the sauce by combining all the ingredients together in a small bowl, mix gently then set aside.

Cut the haddock and prawns into small pieces. Place in a food processor with the almonds, ham, garlic and ginger and whizz until finely chopped. Add the oil, cornflour, salt and soy sauce and process until the mixture sticks together.

Take a teaspoon of the mixture and form it into a ball. Repeat with the rest of the mixture. Shallow-fry the balls, in batches, for 3–4 minutes until golden. Then transfer them to a

Not only are markets fascinating places to visit, they provide a truly local ambiance and an indispensable guide to the indigenous fresh produce which is vital for creating rich and interesting flavours in cooking. Herbs, particularly in France and Italy, are readily available from local markets. They look visually alluring and taste marvellous when added to soups and vegetable dishes.

pre-heated plate covered with kitchen paper and keep warm.

Divide the sauce among 4 bowls and place on individual plates. Surround the bowl of sauce with a few leaves of lettuce, mint and coriander, and divide the hot fish balls among the plates.

The way to eat this dish is to tear off a piece of lettuce leaf and place a fish ball and a mint or coriander leaf on it. Roll up the lettuce leaf like a small green parcel. Dip one end into the sauce and eat.

FRESH HERB PASTA
WITH PESTO

This lovely green-flecked egg pasta is mixed with chopped fresh herbs. You can use a mixture of several compatible herbs like parsley, chervil and thyme, or use just one such as rosemary, tarragon or sage to give the pasta a distinctive flavour. Unless I'm very short of time, I make pasta by hand because I enjoy handling the soft dough. If you use a pasta machine, roll out the pasta on its thinnest setting. Pesto is, of course, the definitive sauce for pasta, but a well-blended herb butter is almost as delicious.

SERVES 2–4
140g (5oz) plain unbleached flour
¼ teaspoon salt
2–3 tablespoons chopped fresh herbs:
parsley, chervil, tarragon, rosemary,
thyme, sage
1 tablespoon olive oil
1 egg, beaten
1–2 teaspoons water as necessary
extra virgin olive oil
freshly ground black pepper
pesto sauce (see page 36)

Sift the flour and salt into a bowl. Stir in the herbs and olive oil and mix to a dough with the egg, adding sufficient water as necessary. Knead the dough together into a ball when it should start to feel elastic. Alternatively, mix all the ingredients in a food processor, then gather the dough together to form a ball.

Turn the dough on to a floured board and knead for 10 minutes. Cover dough with the upturned bowl and rest it for 45 minutes.

Cut the dough in half and roll out each piece until it is as thin as possible. Drape the dough over the back of a chair, rope or broomhandle and leave to dry for 20–30 minutes.

Fold the pasta into a loose roll and cut into strips according to your preference. Tagliatelle is cut to a width of 6mm (¼in), fettuccine is cut 3mm (⅛in). Unroll the folds of pasta so that they do not stick together and leave covered by a cloth until ready to cook.

Cook the herb pasta in plenty of boiling salted water. It will need only 2–3 minutes: it is cooked when it rises to the top of the pan. Drain well and return to the pan with some extra virgin olive oil and freshly ground black pepper. Toss well.

Serve in dishes with the pesto sauce spooned over the pasta.

COURGETTE AND SORREL
SOUP WITH ALMOND AND
CHIVE SABLES

As soon as I'd devised this soup I wondered why I'd not thought of it before. For during the summer months, both courgettes and sorrel grow in super-abundance and their flavours are truly complementary.

SERVES 5–6
60g (2oz) butter
1–2 spring onions, chopped
500g (1lb) young courgettes, trimmed and
sliced
a sliver of garlic
a bay leaf
120g (4oz) sorrel leaves, washed, drained
and roughly shredded
300ml (½ pint) well-flavoured chicken or
vegetable stock
150ml (¼ pint) double cream
milk
salt
GARNISH
4–6 tablespoons double cream
1 teaspoon long shreds of lemon zest
ALMOND AND MARJORAM SABLES
60g (2oz) butter, softened
1 teaspoon finely chopped chives
120g (4oz) plain flour
30g (1oz) ground almonds
Parmesan cheese, grated
1 egg yolk
1–3 tablespoons cold water
30g (1oz) split blanched almonds

First make the almond and chive sablés: in a mixing bowl, cream the butter with the chives. Sift the flour and ground almonds into a bowl and stir in the Parmesan cheese. Rub in the chive butter and mix to a soft dough with the egg yolk and water.

Take a teaspoonful of dough and gently roll it into a ball on a floured surface. Slightly flatten the ball into an oval shape on a buttered baking sheet and press a split almond into the top. Make the remaining sablés in the same way (there should be 24–30). Bake in a moderate oven (180°C, 350°F, gas mark 4) for

15–20 minutes until the biscuits are golden and crisp. Cool on the baking sheet for 2 minutes, then transfer to a wire rack. Serve the sablés cold or warm.

Melt the butter in a saucepan and stir in the spring onions, courgettes and garlic until coated with butter. Add the bay leaf, cover the pan and cook over moderate heat for 10–15 minutes until the courgettes are tender. Remove the bay leaf, and stir in the roughly shredded sorrel with the stock. Cook for 4–5 minutes until the sorrel has wilted then purée the contents of the pan in a food processor. Add the cream and pour through a sieve back into the pan. Reheat gently, and thin with milk to the desired consistency. Season with salt.

Pour the soup into bowls and garnish with some double cream and shreds of lemon zest. Serve accompanied by the sablés.

TOMATO TARTS
WITH HERB BUTTER

The contrast of textures in these thin crisp pastry tarts covered with slices of hot tomato and herbs is very good indeed.

SERVES 6
250g (9oz) prepared puff pastry
90g (3oz) butter, softened
2 tablespoons finely chopped mixed herbs
– basil, parsley, thyme, chives
a little finely grated lemon zest
a squeeze of lemon juice
3 large marmande or beefsteak tomatoes
salt and freshly milled black pepper

Divide the pastry into 6 pieces and roll out each piece on a floured board to make a 15cm (6in) round.

Cream the butter with the herbs, lemon zest and juice until well combined. Spread the herb butter over each round of pastry and place on a sheet of baking parchment on a baking sheet. Slice the tomatoes very thinly and place 3 slices, slightly overlapping, on each pastry round. Season with salt and pepper.

Bake in a moderately hot oven (200°C, 400°F, gas mark 6) for 15–20 minutes until the pastry is crisp and golden. Serve straight away.

FISH AND SHELLFISH

The delicate nature of most fish and shellfish is invariably flattered by the presence
of an appropriate herb. Fish cooks quickly and is ready to eat
as soon as the flesh is opaque and the bone separates easily.
Consequently fragile and delicate herbs such as sorrel, mint and dill
often make the best partners for fish since they require
only brief cooking to release their flavour.
Once you become used to cooking fish with herbs you will find them indispensable.
A bouquet garni added to the court bouillon *(poaching liquid)*
not only adds a uniquely delicious flavour to the fish, but the strained liquor can
then be reduced to make a fumet, *or base, for a sauce with the simple addition*
of a knob of butter or a spoonful of cream.
Many of the classic sauces that accompany fish depend on just a few sprigs
of a fresh herb and a dash of wine for their character; the results have a subtle flavour and
vibrancy that is unequalled. Herb butters such as lime and chives, or tomato and basil,
added as a garnish to a fish dish just before serving produce a delicious
lift in flavour. The butter bathes the fish in a thin layer of glistening moisture
and the finely chopped herbs soak into the flakes of flesh, giving it a fine tang
that is far removed from the sickroom image of plainly cooked fish.
When cooking fish with herbs it is instructive and inspirational to study other
cuisines where fish comprises a large part of the daily diet.
The marinated fish cookery of Scandinavia and the Pacific, for example,
both of which make good use of herbs,
includes the superb dishes of gravad lax *and* ceviche, *which highlight*
some of the less familiar herbs such as dill, fennel and coriander.

PREVIOUS PAGE *left to right* BOILED LOBSTER WITH HERB MAYONNAISE, *page 23;*
SEAFOOD SALAD WITH CITRUS AND FENNEL DRESSING, *page 23.*

BOILED LOBSTER
WITH HERB MAYONNAISE

A freshly-cooked lobster tastes superb served hot or cold, with a richly-flavoured herb mayonnaise. The flavour of the mayonnaise improves if it is made a few hours ahead – in fact, herb mayonnaise is a useful sauce to keep in the refrigerator for 2–3 days.

SERVES 2
2 egg yolks
1 coffeespoon Dijon mustard
75–100ml (3–4fl oz) mild-flavoured olive or sunflower oil, at room temperature
75–100ml (3–4fl oz) grapeseed oil
2–3 tablespoons very finely chopped mixed summer herbs: tarragon, parsley, chervil, chives, basil, marjoram
lemon juice to taste
150ml (¼ pint) crème fraîche or soured cream (optional)
1 live lobster, weighing about 1kg (2¼lb)
sea water or salt
bouquet garni of fresh herbs (see page 87)

Make sure that the bowl and the ingredients for the mayonnaise are at room temperature. Blend the egg yolks with the mustard and very gradually, drop by drop, add the oils, beating in each addition thoroughly. If the mayonnaise gets too thick, beat in a little warm water to thin it. Finally, mix in the herbs and enough lemon juice to adjust the flavour. Spoon into a dish or a lidded jar and chill for 4–8 hours. Just before serving, stir in crème fraîche if desired.

Put the lobster into a deep pot, cover to a depth of 15cm (6in) with seawater or salted water and add the bouquet garni. Bring to the boil and cook for 7 minutes per 450g (1lb) of lobster. For eating cold, remove the lobster and plunge it into ice-cold water to stop the cooking; for serving hot, leave the lobster in the cooking water until ready to serve.

To serve the lobster, place it on its back and cut it lengthways into 2 halves. Discard the feathery fronds in the centre and remove the intestinal tract. Crack the claws and remove the shell to expose the meat. Spoon some herb mayonnaise into the cavity in the shell.

SEAFOOD SALAD WITH CITRUS
AND FENNEL DRESSING

Vary the seafood in this salad according to season and availability. During the summer months, squid, prawns and clams are probably easier to come by. Autumn and winter bring good supplies of excellent mussels, langoustines and shrimps.

SERVES 6–8
170g (6oz) poached baby squid, cut into rings
170g (6oz) each of cooked prawns, mussels, langoustines, gambas or Mediterranean prawns, clams, cockles etc., peeled or on the shell as you wish, to make a total weight of 450–675g (1–1½lb)
DRESSING
3–4 sprigs of fennel
1 clove garlic, halved
½ teaspoon finely grated orange zest
juice of 1 orange
juice of 2 limes or 1 small lemon
75–100ml (3–4fl oz) olive oil
2 tablespoons crème fraîche
salt and freshly milled green peppercorns
GARNISH
sprigs of fennel and heads of fennel flower if available
endive frisée

Once you have prepared the seafood ingredients according to your requirements, place all the seafood together in a large bowl.

Make the dressing by warming the fennel, garlic, orange zest and orange juice in a small pan. Bring almost to the boil, then remove from the heat and allow the flavours to infuse for 15 minutes.

Strain the liquid into a bowl and add the juice of the limes or lemon. Gradually whisk in the oil, then stir in the crème fraîche and season to taste with salt and the freshly milled green peppercorns. Pour the dressing over the seafood and leave to marinate in a cold place for 1–3 hours.

To serve, heap the seafood on to a large platter and garnish with sprigs of fennel and fennel flower and some endive frisée.

SALMON BAKED
WITH A HERB CRUST

A mixture of fine white breadcrumbs and freshly chopped herbs makes an excellent coating for a delicate fish, retaining all the flavour and succulence of the fish during the cooking. Halibut is another fish with a delicate consistency which makes a very good alternative to salmon in this recipe.

SERVES 4
4 × 180g (6oz) salmon steaks
juice of 1 lemon
salt and freshly milled pepper
120g (4oz) fresh white bread with the crusts removed
½ teacup of mixed chopped fresh herbs: parsley, chervil, chives, basil, tarragon, mint.
½ teaspoon finely grated lemon zest
60g (2oz) butter, melted
1–2 tablespoons medium dry white wine

Pat the fish dry with kitchen paper, then sprinkle half the lemon juice over both sides of each salmon steak and season lightly with salt and pepper. Place the fish in a well-buttered ovenproof dish.

Break the bread into the bowl of a food processor, add the herbs and process until the bread has formed crumbs and the mixture is pale green. Add the lemon zest, some salt and pepper, and two-thirds of the butter with the remaining lemon juice. Process again until the mixture lightly binds together – if necessary carefully add a little cold water which should encourage the binding process.

Spoon the herb mixture over the salmon, pressing it down lightly to form an even layer. Pour over the remaining butter and spoon the wine into the dish around the salmon steaks. Cover the fish with a butter paper, or buttered greaseproof. Bake in a moderately hot oven (190°C, 375°F, gas mark 5) for 20–25 minutes or until the salmon is opaque and cooked. Serve straight away. There can be no better accompaniment to this dish than new potatoes tossed in mint-flavoured butter and steamed mangetout peas.

Although tuna is preferable for the grilled fish recipe (bottom left), mackerel could also be used if tuna were unavailable. Fish is always delicious when served with a slightly spicy sauce. Here, coriander provides an excellent accompaniment and a good contrast to the hot green chillis.

GRILLED TUNA FISH WITH COCONUT, LEMON GRASS AND CORIANDER SAUCE

Tuna fish, mahi-mahi and mackerel have a delicious dense, almost meat-like texture which makes them excellent for grilling over charcoal. Their flavour goes particularly well with this delectable Thai-inspired sauce.

SERVES 4
4 tuna steaks
2 lemons
2 tablespoons plain or lovage flavoured sunflower oil
300ml ($\frac{1}{2}$ pint) coconut milk, fresh, tinned or powdered
1 stalk of lemon grass, bruised and cut into short pieces
1 fresh green chilli, halved and seeded
a walnut-size piece of fresh root ginger, peeled and sliced
2 spring onions or 1 clove garlic, chopped
$\frac{1}{2}$ teaspoon Thai or Indonesian *nam pla* (fish sauce)
a hand-sized bunch of fresh coriander
1 teaspoon arrowroot blended with 1 tablespoon cold water
finely grated zest and juice of 1 lime

First you must marinate the fish. Use kitchen paper to dry the fish, then cut the lemons in half, remove the flesh and squeeze it to extract the juice. Reserve the lemon shells for serving the dish later. Mix the lemon juice with the oil and a little salt and pour over both sides of the fish. Set aside in a cool place to marinate for up to 2 hours until ready to cook.

Make the sauce by combining the coconut milk with the lemon grass, chilli, ginger, spring onions, fish sauce and the stalks (plus roots if any) of the coriander in a saucepan. Bring to the boil and simmer for 10–15 minutes until reduced by one-third. Strain the sauce and return to the pan, then add the arrowroot and cook over moderate heat, stirring, until slightly thickened. Remove from the heat and add the lime zest and juice, season with salt, and add the coarsely chopped coriander leaves. Keep the sauce warm.

Grill the fish on both sides, preferably over charcoal but otherwise place the fish under a grill set on high, basting with any remaining marinade while cooking. Serve the fish with some of the sauce spooned into the empty lemon shells and hand the rest separately. Plain boiled rice goes well with this dish as it leaves you to savour all the subtle flavours of the fish and its sauce.

SMOKED SALMON TROUT MOUSSE WITH FENNEL

This creamy-pink well-flavoured mousse is nicest served as a first course with a small salad of young leaves and hot Melba toast.

SERVES 4–6
120g (4oz) smoked salmon trout, sliced
3–4 sprigs of fennel leaves, chopped
120g (4oz) unsalted butter, softened
120g (4oz) clotted cream
$\frac{1}{2}$ teaspoon finely grated orange zest
2 tablespoons orange juice
a good pinch of ground allspice
2–3 teaspoons elderflower vinegar (see page 79) or Pernod
extra sprigs and flowers (if available) of fennel to garnish

Flake the salmon trout into the bowl of a food processor, add the chopped fennel and butter and process until well mixed. Add the cream, orange zest and juice, allspice and vinegar or Pernod and process until well mixed but not too smooth.

Spoon the mousse into a dish and smooth level. Cover and chill for 1–2 hours. Garnish with the sprigs of fennel before serving.

BAY TREE BROCHETTES OF COD WITH YELLOW PEPPERS AND BLACK OLIVES

Instead of cod, any very fresh white fish such as John Dory or monkfish may be used to make this attractive summer dish.

SERVES 4

700–900g (1½–2lb) skinned fillet of cod
1 lemon
1–2 tablespoons clear English or Greek honey
2 tablespoons olive oil
1 tablespoon finely chopped mint leaves
salt and freshly milled black pepper
2 yellow sweet peppers
24–30 stoned black olives
8–12 fresh bay leaves
a little extra olive oil
8 skewers made from stems of fresh bay or wooden skewers
boiled white rice cooked with olive oil, bay leaves and garlic, to serve

Remove any errant bones from the fish, then cut the fillet into 30–40 even-sized pieces.

Wash and dry the lemon, then use a lemon zester to remove long shreds of zest. Place in a wide, shallow bowl and add the strained juice of the lemon, the honey, olive oil and mint. Stir, then check the taste and season lightly if you wish. Add the fish and turn over gently in the marinade until evenly coated. Set aside in a cool place to marinate for 30–60 minutes.

Remove the core and seeds from the peppers and cut into pieces about the same size as the fish. Put in a shallow bowl with the olives and bay leaves and dribble over a little olive oil.

Thread the fish, peppers, olives and bay leaves on to the skewers and place on a lightly oiled grill pan or ovenproof dish. Spoon any surplus marinade over the fish and cook under a high grill, turning the brochettes once, for 5–8 minutes or until the fish is pearly white but still very moist.

Spoon some of the hot rice on to 4 plates and place 2 brochettes beside it on each plate. Spoon the cooking juices over the rice.

SALMON AND DILL FISHCAKES WITH SORREL SAUCE

These very good fish cakes can be made up to a day ahead if kept covered on a floured plate in a cold place.

SERVES 4

450g (1lb) tail piece of salmon
4 tablespoons medium-dry white wine
450g (1lb) old potatoes, peeled and freshly boiled
30g (1oz) butter, softened
1 teaspoon finely chopped dill
1 teaspoon finely chopped chives
$\frac{1}{4}$–$\frac{1}{2}$ teaspoon peeled and finely grated fresh root ginger
$\frac{1}{4}$ teaspoon finely grated lemon zest
salt
seasoned flour
sunflower oil for shallow frying
SORREL SAUCE
120g (4oz) sorrel leaves
30g (1oz) butter
150ml ($\frac{1}{4}$ pint) double cream
1 clove garlic
salt

Place the salmon in an ovenproof dish, pour over the wine and cover with a butter wrapper or buttered greaseproof paper. Bake in a moderate oven (180°C, 350°F, gas mark 4) for 20–30 minutes or until the flesh is opaque and just coming free of the bone.

Set aside to cool, then remove the skin and bones and flake the flesh into a bowl. Add the cooking juices.

Put the potatoes through a 'mouli-légumes', or mash them well, and add to the fish. Add the butter, dill, chives, ginger, lemon zest and salt to taste. Mix gently so that the fish flakes are still discernible. Shape into flat cakes 8–10cm (3–4in) across and 2.5cm (1in) thick. Coat in seasoned flour and store until ready to cook.

To make the sorrel sauce, wash the sorrel leaves in cold water and remove the stalks. Place in a pan over moderate heat with half the butter and stir until the leaves have collapsed into a soft mass. Cook until all the surplus water has evaporated.

Purée the sorrel in a food processor or blender and return to the pan with the cream. Peel the clove of garlic and impale it on a fork. Stir the sauce with the fork over low heat for 2–3 minutes until it has absorbed sufficient garlic flavour, then discard the garlic. Season with salt and add the remaining butter. Keep the sauce warm.

Shallow fry the fish cakes in sunflower oil for 3–4 minutes on each side until golden brown. Serve straight away on hot plates with some sorrel sauce spooned over.

There is no need whatsoever for fresh fish to taste bland. Simple cooking methods like poaching and grilling come into their own and an addition of herbs to the cooking process ensures a lively, appetizing flavour. Often the only extra flourish that is needed can be provided by the addition of fresh lemon juice, a pat of tarragon butter or a spoonful of cream infused with the flowers of chervil or thyme.

CRAB AND BROCCOLI GRATIN WITH CORIANDER LEAVES

The uniquely delicious taste of crabmeat is always enhanced by the flavour of fresh herbs. Although dill, fennel, parsley and tarragon all go well with crabmeat, I find that the oriental flavour of coriander leaves lightens and freshens the taste of this superb shellfish.

SERVES 4
225g (8oz) dressed crab
225g (8oz) broccoli or calabrese
salt
2 bay leaves
45g (1½oz) butter
30g (1oz) plain flour
400ml (14fl oz) single cream or creamy milk
1 teaspoon chopped chives
2 tablespoons chopped coriander leaves
60g (2oz) Gruyère cheese, finely grated
60g (2oz) dryish white breadcrumbs

If possible, separate the white crabmeat from the brown. Break the broccoli or calabrese into bite-size florets; cook in boiling salted water with a bay leaf until tender. Drain well.

Grease four small gratin dishes and divide the brown meat between them. Arrange the broccoli and half the white crab meat on top.

Melt the butter in a saucepan and stir in the flour for 1–2 minutes but do not allow it to change colour. Gradually stir in the cream, add the remaining bay leaf and cook, stirring, for 5–7 minutes until thickened. Discard the bay leaf, and stir in the chives, coriander, half the cheese and the remaining white meat. Check the flavour and add salt if necessary. Divide the sauce between the dishes, spooning it over the broccoli and crabmeat. Mix the remaining cheese with the breadcrumbs and sprinkle over the top of each dish.

Bake in a moderately hot oven (200°C, 400°F, gas mark 6) for 10–15 minutes or until the sauce is bubbling and the topping is golden and crisp.

MEAT, POULTRY AND GAME

Keen cooks quite soon discover that fresh herbs act like a seasoning for meat.
They bring out its true taste and provide an aromatic foil for its rich flavour.
Yet at each stage in the cooking process herbs contribute a subtly different effect.
A joint of beef or a saddle of hare, for instance,
slowly marinaded in a blend of thyme and juniper berries mixed with wine,
yoghurt or fruit juice can produce a sumptuous dish of complex yet harmonious flavours
that quite transforms the separate ingredients.
On the other hand, a purée of garlic crushed with finely chopped rosemary and olive oil
spread over lamb cutlets and chilled for 1–3 hours before grilling or roasting
contributes a fresh, vivid taste to the meat. Similarly, a
chicken or guinea fowl roasted under a crust of herbs mixed
with breadcrumbs develops a delicate herb-infused succulence.
Some herbs best enhance the flavour of meat when added after the cooking, as in an
escalope of veal served with a lemon thyme sauce. If prepared ahead
and stored in the fridge or freezer, such sauces and butters can embellish
the fastest of foods to give an almost instant and flavourful distinction.

PREVIOUS PAGE *left to right* ROAST DUCK WITH A SAUCE OF MORELLO CHERRIES AND HYSSOP, *page 31;*
BAKED SWEET POTATOES WITH CHIVE AND GINGER BUTTER, *page 57.*

ROAST DUCK WITH A SAUCE OF MORELLO CHERRIES AND HYSSOP

A simple roast duck served with a vibrant sauce always makes a good meal. Because my morello tree produces plenty of fruit, I devised this sauce based on them. Nevertheless, sweet red cherries can replace the morellos provided that you sharpen the flavour of the sauce with a little lemon juice.

SERVES 4–6

1.8–2.25kg (4–5lb) oven-ready duckling
1 onion, quartered
salt
5 tablespoons Côtes du Rhône wine
450g (1lb) ripe morello cherries, stoned
juice of 1 orange
45–60g (1½–2oz) light muscovado sugar
4 sprigs of hyssop
1 teaspoon arrowroot
1 tablespoon eau-de-vie de cerises or cold water
a pinch of ground allspice
30g (1oz) butter
cherries and/or sprigs of hyssop, to garnish (optional)

Remove the giblets from the duck and place the onion inside the body cavity. Pat the duck skin dry with kitchen paper and rub in some salt. Place the duck on a rack in a roasting tin and put the giblets in the bottom of the tin.

Roast the duck in a moderately hot oven (190°C, 375°F, gas mark 5) for 1–1¼ hours or until cooked. During the cooking, pour off the surplus fat occasionally and reserve it for other cooking, particularly potato dishes. When the duck is cooked, transfer it to a serving dish and keep warm in a low oven until ready to serve.

Pour off all surplus fat from the roasting tin and add the wine. Cook over high heat for 4 minutes, stirring to incorporate the cooking juices and sediments from the duck. Strain the liquid into a cup and keep warm.

Put the cherries in a saucepan with the orange juice, sugar and 2 sprigs of hyssop. Cook gently until the juice is released from the fruit, then remove from the heat and discard the hyssop. Blend the arrowroot with the eau-de-vie or water and add to the cherries together with the wine stock and the allspice. Cook, stirring, over a moderate heat for 3–5 minutes until the sauce has cleared and thickened. Add the leaves from the remaining sprigs of hyssop and check the flavour of the sauce, adding salt and/or sugar to taste. Remove from the heat and add the butter. When it has melted, spoon some sauce over the duck and serve the rest from a sauce boat.

PORK TENDERLOIN WITH HAM AND LOVAGE

This is delicious served with a crisp green salad for lunch or a picnic. I find one teaspoon of chopped tarragon in place of lovage can be used equally well.

SERVES 4–6

1 pork tenderloin or fillet
60g (2oz) butter, softened
3–4 lovage leaves, finely chopped
1 tablespoon fine white breadcrumbs
120g (4oz) lean cooked ham, thinly sliced
2 tablespoons finely chopped parsley, chives and thyme

Cut the pork in half lengthways and then across to make four pieces. Use a meat mallet to beat each piece of meat until slightly larger and thinner.

Cream the butter with the lovage and the breadcrumbs and spread over three pieces of the meat. Arrange the sliced ham, cut to fit, on top. Layer the pieces on top of each other with the plain piece on top, pressing them gently together. Tie with string in 3 places, season lightly all over and then roll the meat in the chopped mixed herbs and wrap in lightly oiled foil.

Roast in a moderately hot oven (190°C, 375°F, gas mark 5) for 35–40 minutes or until the meat is cooked.

Remove from the oven and allow to cool. Then unwrap and chill well before cutting the meat into slices. You will find that this dish slices easily when chilled.

FILLET OF BEEF WITH JUNIPER BERRIES AND CRIQUE ARDECHOISE

The fruity wine-like taste of juniper berries make them a perfect flavouring for many game and beef dishes. The crique ardèchoise *is a straw potato pancake made with finely chopped garlic and parsley.*

SERVES 4

4 beef fillet steaks
6 juniper berries
6 black peppercorns
90g (3oz) butter
150ml (¼ pint) red Côtes du Rhône wine
90ml (3fl oz) beef or vegetable stock
CRIQUE
450g (1lb) maincrop potatoes
1–2 cloves garlic, very finely chopped
1 tablespoon finely chopped parsley
salt
sunflower oil for shallow frying
4 sprigs of flat leaf parsley

Place the steaks on a plate. Crush the juniper berries and peppercorns with a pestle in a mortar until fairly fine. Rub the mixture into all the surfaces of the meat, then set aside in a cold place for 1–2 hours.

To make the *crique*, peel the potatoes and grate into a bowl. Stir in the garlic, parsley and salt. Divide the mixture into 4 rounds and shallow fry in the oil, allowing about 5 minutes on each side. The cooked *crique* should be golden brown and crisp on the outside.

Meanwhile, melt half the butter in a shallow pan and fry the steaks on both sides to your satisfaction. Transfer the meat to a hot dish and keep warm. Add the wine and stock to the pan, stirring and scraping with a wooden spoon to incorporate all the pan juices, and bring to the boil. Simmer fast until reduced by half, then strain into a small pan and keep warm. Just before serving beat the remaining butter into the sauce.

Cut each fillet steak into three or four slices and arrange on a hot plate. Spoon over some of the sauce and place the *crique* beside it. Garnish with a sprig of parsley and serve.

The combination of garlic and herbs is a classic association that has its roots in French cooking.

RABBIT PIE
WITH PARSLEY CREAM

A traditional English rabbit pie has long been associated with harvest time when meals were carried out into the fields so that farmworkers could eat in the shade of a tree. This pie is good at any time of the year, but late summer, around harvest time, seems particularly appropriate.

SERVES 4–6
1 medium-size rabbit, jointed
salt and freshly milled pepper
60g (2oz) butter
2 spring onions or 1 slim clove garlic,
chopped
5 tablespoons medium dry white wine
such as a riesling or a chardonnay
6 tablespoons water
2 sprigs of thyme
2 teaspoons cornflour
300ml (½ pint) crème fraîche or double
cream
2–3 tablespoons finely chopped parsley
225g (8oz) puff or shortcrust pastry
egg yolk, to glaze

Wash the rabbit and dry with kitchen paper. Season the joints of meat with salt and pepper.

Melt the butter in a frying pan and lightly brown the rabbit joints all over. Stir in the spring onions or garlic for 1 minute, then add the wine and 5 tablespoons of the water. Transfer the contents of the pan to a pie dish and add the sprigs of thyme. Cover with a sheet of foil, sealing the edges well. Cook in a moderately hot oven (190°C, 375°F, gas mark 5) for 30 minutes. Remove the dish from the oven. Raise the oven temperature to 200°C, 400°F, gas mark 6. Remove the sprigs of thyme from the pie dish and discard. Blend the cornflour with the remaining water in a bowl and mix in the crème fraîche, the parsley and cooking juices from the pie dish. Pour this over the rabbit and, if desired, place a pie funnel in the middle of the dish.

On a floured board, roll out the pastry to fit the dish, lay it over the dish and trim the edges. Make a steam vent over the pie funnel, or make 2–3 vents in the pastry. Use any trimmings to make the pastry leaves and berries and arrange on the pie crust. Brush the pastry with egg yolk before heating in the oven.

Bake the pie for 25–30 minutes until the pastry is golden brown and crisp. Serve hot.

SIMPLE ROAST CHICKEN
STUFFED WITH HERBS

It is a truism that the simpler the cooking style, the more important the ingredients. Chicken roasted with just butter and herbs requires a high quality roasting bird, preferably maize-fed and free-range or a poulet de Bresse *to bring out the best in the method.*

SERVES 4–6
1 × 1.5–2kg (3–4lb) roasting chicken,
without giblets
a bundle of fresh mixed herbs: parsley,
chives, tarragon, fennel, thyme, marjoram
or whatever is available
60g (2oz) butter, softened
60–90ml (2–3fl oz) medium dry white
wine
60–90ml (2–3fl oz) water or fresh
vegetable stock
1 teaspoon finely chopped fresh herbs

Place the chicken in a roasting tin. Stuff the bundle of herbs into the cavity of the chicken and spread the butter over the breast. Roast in a moderately hot oven (190°C, 375°F, gas mark 5) for 1–1½ hours or until the juices run clear when the bird is pierced below the joint on the leg. During cooking, baste the breast with the fat in the tin now and again.

Transfer the chicken to a hot serving dish and set aside in a warm place for at least 15 minutes so that the meat will be easier to carve. Meanwhile, make the gravy: pour off the surplus fat from the roasting tin and add the wine and water or stock. Boil fast on top of the stove for 3–4 minutes, scraping the pan with a wooden spoon to incorporate the cooking juices and sediment. Remove from the heat. Just before serving, add the chopped herbs to the gravy and bring almost to the boil.

BUTTERFLIED LAMB
A LA MAROC

This is one of the classic lamb dishes of the Maghreb, the territory that stretches from Tunisia to Morocco. The flavours of the blend of spices and herbs seep into the meat while it marinates for 3–5 hours.

SERVES 6–8
1 leg of lamb, boned
1 teaspoon black peppercorns
1½ teaspoons cumin seeds
1½ teaspoons coriander seeds
1 tablespoon sweet paprika
3 cloves garlic, finely chopped or crushed
1–2 tablespoons olive oil
1–2 tablespoons water
2 handfuls of coriander leaves, chopped

Spread out the boned leg of lamb on a flat platter or wooden board and, if necessary, make incisions in the meat to ensure that it is almost the same thickness all over.

Grind together the peppercorns, cumin and coriander seeds in a pestle and mortar, or use an electric coffee mill but do not make the mixture too fine. Mix with the paprika, garlic, olive oil, water and coriander leaves to make a spreadable paste.

Rub and spread the paste over both surfaces of the leg of lamb, making sure that it penetrates all the crevices. Set aside in a cold place to marinate for 3–5 hours.

Cook the lamb either over charcoal or under a grill set on high, allowing about 15 minutes for each side, or until the meat is cooked to your satisfaction. The lamb is most delicious when still pink in the centre.

Remove from the heat and place on a wooden platter. Cut into thick slices for serving with a fresh green salad.

To dry small quantities of herbs place the leaves in a paper bag before drying. An electric food dryer is also an efficient way of drying several herbs at the same time.

GASCON LAMB WITH
GARLIC AND ROSEMARY

Right across the south of France lamb is studded with garlic and sometimes thyme, rosemary, herbes de Provence or fillets of anchovy. The joint is then roasted until the meat – indeed, the whole kitchen – is perfumed with this heady mixture.

SERVES 8–10
1 × 2kg (4–5lb) leg of lamb
1 small head of garlic, each clove cut into
slices
3–4 sprigs of rosemary
salt and freshly milled pepper
goose fat or softened butter

Place the lamb on a wooden carving board and make sure that all the tough outer skin and any surplus fat has been removed. With a sharp-pointed knife, make a cut into the skin of the meat. Push a sliver of garlic and 2–3 rosemary leaves into the incision. Repeat all over the lamb, then place it in a roasting tin. Season with salt and pepper and smear with goose fat or butter.

Roast the meat in a moderately hot oven (200°C, 400°F, gas mark 6) for about 1½ hours or until the meat is cooked to your liking. Transfer the lamb to a carving dish or board and leave to rest in a warm place for at least 20 minutes before carving.

QUAIL COOKED IN VINE LEAVES WITH PESTO

The small delicious quail is now more commonly farmed than reared in the wild. The bird has been wrapped and roasted in vine leaves for centuries in France; however, a thin layer of pesto or a herb butter (see page 71) spread over the meat and under the vine leaf does wonders for the flavour.

SERVES 2–4
8–12 vine leaves, fresh and blanched or
brined and rinsed
4 oven ready quail
1 tablespoon olive oil
PESTO
100g (3½oz) basil leaves
8 tablespoons olive oil
30g (1oz) pine kernels
2 medium size cloves garlic, chopped
¼ teaspoon salt (optional)
60g (2oz) Parmesan cheese, freshly grated

Make the pesto by measuring the basil, olive oil, pine kernels, garlic and salt into a blender or food processor and whizzing until you have an even paste. Alternatively, pound the ingredients together with a pestle in a mortar. Gradually work in the freshly grated Parmesan cheese. Spoon the sauce into a dish (any left over from this recipe is best saved for serving with hot pasta).

Place 2–3 vine leaves, slightly over-lapping, in a lightly oiled gratin dish. Spread pesto all over the body of one quail, place on the vine leaves and wrap them round to enclose the bird. Repeat with the other quail. Brush the parcels with olive oil.

Roast the quail in a moderate oven (180°C, 350°F, gas mark 4) for 35–45 minutes or until cooked. Serve with boiled new potatoes.

For cooking over a wood fire or barbeque, wrap the vine-clad quail in foil and cook, turning them now and again, for 45–60 minutes depending upon the heat of the fire.

An Italian delicatessen is invariably a good source for buying fresh Parmesan cheese.

VEAL AND SAGE ROLLS

Saltimbocca, *the Italian name of this simple but very good dish, means 'leaps into the mouth'. Use slim young leaves of sage for the best flavour.*

SERVES 6
700–900g (1½–2lb) veal or turkey escalopes
salt and freshly milled pepper
200g (7oz) prosciutto or Parma ham
about 24 young sage leaves
3–4 tablespoons seasoned flour
60g (2oz) butter
2 tablespoons olive oil
150ml (¼ pint) dry white Italian wine,
Chianti or Marsala
cubes of white day-old bread for croûtons
extra olive oil or butter for frying

If necessary, beat the escalopes between two layers of plastic film until large enough to cut into a total of 24 pieces. Season the meat lightly with salt and pepper and cover each piece with prosciutto, cut slightly smaller. Place a sage leaf in the centre, roll up the meat and secure each roll with a wooden cocktail stick. Set the rolls aside in a cold place until ready to cook.

Toss the veal or turkey rolls in seasoned flour. Heat the butter and oil in a frying pan until foaming, then shallow-fry the veal rolls for 5–7 minutes (less for turkey) until golden-brown all over.

Add the wine to the pan, cover and cook for 5–8 minutes until the rolls are cooked right through. Meanwhile, fry the bread cubes in butter or olive oil to make the croûtons.

Transfer the meat to a hot serving dish and remove the cocktail sticks. Cook the pan juices over high heat until syrupy, then spoon over the meat and serve with the croûtons.

The classic Italian combination of veal and sage is a delicious one. There are several different varieties of sage, each with its own distinctive colour, flavour and texture. All varieties are particularly delicious when used to flavour savoury dishes and sage butter is a good accompaniment to pork and veal sausages.

PASTA, RICE, EGGS AND CHEESE

Many centuries ago the Italians discovered the delicious combination of herbs
with pasta and rice dishes. Both these staple foods
have a fundamentally bland taste which herbs enliven in a dramatic way.
Some of the most delicious results are achieved by adding fresh herbs,
like finely chopped sage or thyme, to the raw pasta dough itself – a perfect example
of how herbs can elevate the taste of a simple dish to Lucullan heights.
Even plain pasta cooked in boiling salted water with a large bouquet garni of
fresh herbs gains in flavour. But my favourite method
is to return freshly cooked pasta to the pan with some very finely chopped garlic,
a large lump of butter, some olive oil and a handful of fresh chopped herbs. Stir over
moderate heat until all the pasta is flecked with the buttery herbs
and serve straight away with a good seasoning of milled black pepper and
plenty of freshly grated Parmesan cheese.
Freshly boiled rice can be given the same treatment with equally good results.
The Thai-inspired method of adding lots of chopped coriander leaves, some crushed
garlic and a couple of beaten eggs while you stir the mixture over low heat makes a
lovely supper dish or a separate course.
Certain herbs, notably those with an aniseed flavour such as chervil, dill, fennel
and tarragon have an affinity with egg and cheese dishes.
The digestive properties of the herbs appear to lighten the effect of
the rich ingredients. Cheese dishes are always enhanced by the presence of garlic
or chives and nobody could deny that an omelette fines herbes
with its rich flavour of parsley, chervil, chives and
tarragon is far more satisfying than a plain version that is sadly herbless.

PREVIOUS PAGE *left to right* TEA EGGS IN A GREEN NEST, *page 41;*

WILD RICE SALAD WITH OEUFS EN GELÉE À L'ESTRAGON, *page 41;*

TAGLIATELLE WITH TOMATO AND BASIL SALSA, *page 42.*

WILD RICE SALAD WITH OEUFS EN GELEE A L'ESTRAGON

The eggs can be prepared some hours ahead. This dish makes a very good light luncheon or a first course to a summer meal.

SERVES 4
OEUFS EN GELEE
4 eggs
2 tablespoons fino sherry
3 sprigs of tarragon
600ml (1 pint) liquid well-flavoured aspic
½ small red sweet pepper, skinned and diced
2 miniature gherkins, halved
4 slices of cooked ham
SALAD
115g (4oz) wild rice
325ml (12fl oz) cold water
1 clove garlic
2 bay leaves
2 slices of lemon
½ teaspoon salt
DRESSING
1 tablespoon hazelnut oil
1 tablespoon mild olive oil
1–2 teaspoons lemon juice
½ teaspoon finely grated lemon zest
a handful of oak-leaf lettuce, to garnish

Poach the eggs until the whites are set and the yolks are still liquid, then drain and cover with cold water. Gently warm the sherry with 2 sprigs of tarragon, then set aside for 10 minutes to infuse. Strain the sherry into the liquid aspic and pour a 5mm (¼in) layer into the bottom of each of 4 oval or round 150ml (¼ pint) metal or china moulds. Chill until set.

Arrange some tarragon leaves, diced red pepper and half a gherkin cut into a fan shape on the layer of set aspic. Spoon a little liquid aspic on top and chill until set. Trim each poached egg to a neat shape and dry well on kitchen paper, then place an egg in each mould and spoon over aspic jelly to cover. Chill until almost set, then place a slice of ham trimmed to fit on top of the aspic and spoon over the remaining jelly. Chill until set.

Measure the wild rice and water into a pan, add the garlic, bay leaves, slices of lemon and salt and bring to the boil. Cover the pan and cook over low heat for 50–60 minutes until the rice is tender. Pour off any surplus liquid and discard the garlic, bay leaves and slices of lemon from the pan of rice.

Mix the oils and lemon juice and zest into the rice and season with salt. Set the wild rice aside, covered, until cool.

To serve, dip each mould briefly into hot water and unmould on to an individual plate. Spoon some of the rice salad beside each *oeuf en gelée* and garnish with oak-leaf lettuce.

POTTED CHESHIRE CHEESE WITH WALNUTS AND SAGE

Potted cheese is a traditional British dish made by blending finely grated cheese with softened butter, fresh herbs and wine. Cheshire cheese is usually potted with sherry and Wensleydale cheese with port, but other wines like a dry Madeira or even a Malmsey go equally well.

SERVES 4
120g (4oz) unsalted butter, softened
a pinch of cayenne pepper
3–4 sage leaves, finely chopped
260g (9oz) Cheshire cheese, finely grated
4–5 tablespoons Fino sherry
30g (1oz) shelled walnuts, chopped
GARNISH
2–3 leaves of sage
a few walnut halves

Blend the butter with the cayenne pepper and the chopped sage. Gradually work in the cheese with the sherry and chopped walnuts until well combined.

Spoon the mixture into a stone pot or jar, or a pottery bowl, and smooth level. Garnish with sage leaves and walnut halves and store in a cold place until required. Serve with warm bread or hot biscuits and celery.

If covered with a thin layer of clarified butter, potted cheese will store in a refrigerator or a cold larder for up to 1 month.

TEA EGGS IN A GREEN NEST

My friend Dr Yan-Kit So, the leading authority on Chinese cooking, has provided the traditional method for preparing quails' eggs.

SERVES 6
24 quails' eggs
1 tablespoon jasmine tea leaves
300ml (½ pint) water
salt
1 tablespoon light soy sauce
1 teaspoon sugar
6 segments of star anise
2.5cm (1in) cinnamon stick
2 tablespoons hazelnut oil
2 tablespoons safflower or sunflower oil
a squeeze of lime or lemon juice
freshly milled coriander seeds and green or white peppercorns
6 handfuls of small young salad leaves or *mesclun*

Place the eggs in a pan and cover with cold water. Bring slowly to the boil and cook for 1 minute. Remove from the heat, tip into a colander and refresh under cold running water – this makes the eggs easier to peel later.

Boil the tea leaves in the water for about 5 minutes to extract the flavour. Strain the tea into a pan large enough to hold the eggs in a single layer. Add a good pinch of salt, the soy sauce, sugar, star anise and cinnamon stick.

Gently crack the shells to create a network of fine cracks. Put the cracked eggs in the pan with the tea infusion and, if necessary, add water to ensure the eggs are covered. Gently bring to the boil, then lower the heat and simmer, covered, for 20–25 minutes. Remove from the heat and leave the eggs in the liquid for about 6 hours or overnight.

When ready to serve, drain the eggs and remove the shells. Make a dressing by mixing the oils with the lime juice, some milled coriander and pepper and a little salt. Gently toss the salad leaves in the dressing and arrange the leaves to resemble a nest on each of 6 small plates. Divide the eggs among the plates, placing them in the centre of each nest. Serve straight away.

SAFFRON ORZO WITH FRESH BAY LEAVES AND LEMON

Orzo is the rice-shaped pasta from Calabria – the most southern toe of Italy. Orzo is delicious served quite plain, though in this luxurious version the slim oval pasta is cooked with saffron, cream and bay leaves and dressed with lemon juice. It makes a very fine dish that is splendid served on its own or as an accompaniment to grilled meat.

SERVES 6–8
450g (1lb) orzo
salt
30g (1oz) butter
1 tablespoon finely chopped onion
a sliver of garlic, finely chopped
2 generous pinches of high quality saffron threads
2 tablespoons hot water
150ml (¼ pint) double cream
6 fresh bay leaves
finely grated zest and juice of 1 lemon
sprigs of fresh bay leaves, to garnish

Cook the orzo in plenty of boiling salted water for 8–12 minutes until almost tender. Drain, reserving one-quarter of the cooking liquor.

Melt the butter in a pan, add the onion and the garlic and stir over a moderate heat for 4–6 minutes until soft and translucent.

Meanwhile, place the saffron on a saucer and warm in a low oven or under a low grill for 2–3 minutes. Remove from the heat, add the hot water and stir together for 3 minutes until the water starts to take on the distinctive deep yellow colour of saffron.

Add the saffron threads and liquid to the onion with the cream and bay leaves and stir over the heat for 5 minutes. Add the orzo and cook together, stirring, for 5–10 minutes, adding some of the orzo cooking liquid as necessary, until the orzo is tender and has taken on the colour of the saffron. Add salt to taste and discard the bay leaves.

Spoon the orzo on to a hot serving dish. Squeeze lemon juice over the orzo and sprinkle long slim shreds of lemon zest on top. Garnish the dish with fresh bay leaves.

TAGLIATELLE WITH TOMATO AND BASIL SALSA

This luscious combination of hot buttery pasta and a cool aromatic sauce is exceptionally good. Serve in generous amounts as a main course or in smaller portions as a preface to a summer meal.

SERVES 4
225g (8oz) plain tagliatelle
225g (8oz) tagliatelle verde
100g (3½oz) unsalted butter
freshly milled black pepper
SALSA
450g (1lb) ripe fleshy tomatoes
1 clove garlic, crushed
100ml (4fl oz) basil flavoured olive oil (see page 86)
a small handful of basil leaves
salt

Prepare the salsa first. Immerse the tomatoes, one at a time, in boiling water and leave for ½ minute. Remove, nick the skin with the point of a knife and then plunge into ice-cold water to prevent the tomato from cooking. Skin and deseed the tomatoes, dice the flesh neatly and place in a nylon sieve to drain.

Mix the garlic in a bowl with the oil and half the basil leaves snipped into shreds. Stir in the diced tomato and season with salt.

Cook the tagliatelle until *al dente*. Drain it and return to the pan with the butter. When the butter has melted, stir until the pasta is evenly coated, then turn on to a hot serving dish. Spoon over the salsa, garnish with basil and season with freshly milled black pepper.

WILD MUSHROOM RISOTTO WITH NASTURTIUM BUTTER

The slightly peppery flavour of nasturtium flower butter seems to have a natural affinity with rice and pasta. Like all herb butters, it can be stored for 1–2 weeks in the refrigerator or for 1–2 months in the freezer.

SERVES 3–4
90g (3oz) butter
1 red onion, chopped
1 clove garlic, chopped
225g (8oz) Italian arborio or risotto rice
150ml (¼ pint) dry white wine
300–450ml (½–¾ pint) chicken or well-flavoured vegetable stock
120–225g (4–8oz) wild mushrooms, trimmed and cleaned
salt and freshly milled black pepper
a little extra wine
1 tablespoon flat-leaf parsley leaves
few extra nasturtium flowers, to garnish
NASTURTIUM BUTTER
30 nasturtium flowers, assorted colours
90g (3oz) butter, softened
lemon juice, to taste

To make the nasturtium butter, inspect the nasturtium flowers for any insects, remove the stalks and use scissors to snip the flowers into small pieces. Blend the butter with the chopped flowers and add lemon juice to taste. Spoon into a small dish and set aside.

Melt half the other butter in a heavy-based pan and cook the onion and garlic until soft. Stir in the rice and when it is translucent, add the wine. Cook, stirring, until all the liquid has been absorbed. Add the stock, a ladleful at a time, and let each addition be absorbed by the rice before adding the next.

Meanwhile, soften the wild mushrooms in the remaining butter. Add to the rice with some salt and pepper and cook the risotto until the rice is tender.

Add a splash of extra wine and stir in the parsley leaves. Turn the risotto on to a hot serving dish and spoon over some of the nasturtium butter. Garnish with nasturtium flowers and serve.

RICOTTA AND OREGANO RAVIOLI WITH WALNUT BUTTER

Eating in San Francisco is invariably a treat. This pasta dish is derived from a fine meal at the Postrio restaurant near Union Square.

SERVES 4
PASTA DOUGH
120–140g (4–5oz) plain unbleached flour
¼ teaspoon salt
1 size-2 egg
1 egg yolk
2 teaspoons olive oil
FILLING
60g (2oz) butter
½–1 teaspoon finely chopped oregano leaves
340g (12oz) ricotta cheese
1 egg
salt and freshly milled black pepper
30–55g (1–2oz) Parmesan cheese, freshly grated
WALNUT BUTTER
60g (2oz) butter
60g (2oz) walnut halves or pieces

Sift 120g (4oz) of the flour and the salt into a wide, shallow bowl and add the egg beaten with the egg yolk and the olive oil. Mix well, adding just a little extra flour, if necessary, until you have a smooth dough. Shape into a ball and knead on a floured surface for 3–5 minutes until the dough is elastic. Wrap the dough in plastic film and refrigerate for 30 minutes–1 hour.

To make the filling, melt the butter with the oregano and mix into the ricotta with the egg and salt and pepper to taste.

Roll out the dough on a very lightly floured surface until it is very thin. Cut into long narrow strips about 10cm (4in) wide. Fold each strip in half lengthways, then open out again. Place a teaspoon of the filling just below the folded line along the strip every 5cm (2in). Brush the exposed dough lightly with cold water, fold over the strip to enclose the filling and press gently with your fingertips to exclude air from each ravioli pocket. Cut into squares around the mounds of filling using a toothed pasta wheel. Place the filled ravioli on a floured plate or board, cover with a cloth and keep in a cold place until ready to cook.

Poach the ravioli in boiling salted water, in batches, for 4–8 minutes until they rise to the surface. Remove with a slotted spoon and arrange on 4 individual hot gratin dishes. Sprinkle with Parmesan cheese and place under grill until melted.

To make the walnut butter, heat the butter until foaming and stir in the walnuts for 1–2 minutes. Spoon over the ravioli and serve.

OEUFS EN COCOTTE
WITH CHIVES AND HAM

This is a slight adaptation of a lovely little dish of baked eggs from the famous Troigros brothers of Roanne.

SERVES 4
4 new-laid eggs
150ml ($\frac{1}{4}$ pint) double cream
salt and freshly milled black pepper
30g (1oz) raw cured ham such as Bayonne or Parma, diced
$\frac{1}{2}$ tablespoon finely chopped chives
15g ($\frac{1}{2}$oz) butter

Carefully separate the eggs, keeping the yolks whole. Place the whites in a mixing bowl and put each of the yolks in a saucer.

Mix the cream with the egg whites, season with a little salt and beat with a whisk for 30 seconds. Stir in the ham and the chives.

Heat four 75ml (2$\frac{1}{2}$fl oz) ovenproof cocotte dishes in a moderately hot oven (200°C, 400°F, gas mark 6) for a few minutes. Divide the butter between them and place the dishes on a baking tray. Pour the cream mixture into the dishes and bake for 1–3 minutes, or until the custard begins to set.

Remove the dishes from the oven and slip an egg yolk into each, season lightly with pepper and bake for a further 2–3 minutes. Remove from the oven – the eggs will continue to cook in the heat of the dish for a few minutes. Serve straight away.

Goat's cheese coated or gently sprinkled with a variety of herbs such as chopped chives, rosemary, marjoram, thyme, garlic or parsley not only looks spectacular but is imbued with a richly aromatic flavour. Greek cooking favours wrapping the cheese in vine leaves, while the French apply charcoal dust, black peppercorns or chestnut leaves for flavour and decorative effect.

GOATS' CHEESE GRILLED IN VINE LEAVES WITH MARJORAM AND THYME FLOWERS

This is a wonderful mid-summer way to eat freshly drained mild-flavoured goats' cheeses. Choose cheese that is 4–6 days old and that is firm enough to withstand the heat of the grill. Serve the hot cheese with a round loaf of good-tasting country bread like a pain de siegle.

SERVES 4
8–12 flowering sprigs of marjoram and thyme (at other times of the year use non-flowering sprigs)
4 round goats' cheeses
salt and freshly milled black pepper
garlic-flavoured olive oil
16–20 young tender vine leaves
crusty bread, to serve

Arrange 2 sprigs of the herbs on each cheese. Season lightly with salt and pepper and dribble some olive oil over each one. Place each cheese on 3–4 overlapping vine leaves and wrap up like a parcel. Leave the cheeses in a cold place until ready to cook.

Cook the vine-wrapped cheeses on a grid over a charcoal grill, allowing 3–5 minutes for each side. The vine leaves may singe in places but that does not matter. Serve the cheese straight away: unwrap the vine leaves, trickle a little more olive oil on top and eat the cheese with the bread. The inner vine leaves are usually tender enough to eat with the cheese, but discard the outer singed ones.

SALADS AND VEGETABLES

One of the joys of growing your own herbs is to be able to nip out into the garden
to gather a handful of leaves, and to return indoors
to create the freshest, most delectable salad ever.
Rocket leaves, a few sorrel shoots and some sprigs of chervil, fennel and claytonia
are all that you need as a base. For a dressing,
combine a few leaves of tarragon, coriander, basil and lemon balm and snip
some chives and parsley into a garlic-flavoured oil blended with a little
elderflower vinegar. Toss everything together and delight in the end result.
There are times when all cooks need to preserve fresh herbs from the garden
or the market in tip-top condition. Standing the stalks in water
in a cool place works well for 8–12 hours.
For longer storage, wrap the herbs in a damp cloth or place in a roomy plastic bag
and keep in the crisper of the fridge for 1–2 days. Many herbs
will store for up to a week when added, finely chopped, to virgin olive oil, crème fraîche
or yoghurt to make a base for a salad dressing or a sauce for vegetables.
A salad composed entirely of herbs is a fairly exotic mix.
More commonly the herbs are mixed with other young leaves such as lettuce or endive.
And it is, of course, also worthwhile to employ herbs as a
flavouring for cooked vegetable dishes. Try steaming summer vegetables like
baby carrots and sweet peppers on a bed of bay leaves or thyme.
Stuff courgettes and mange-tout peas with a mixture of finely chopped herbs
and freshly drained cheese. Or add their flavour to smooth
vegetable purées and garnish with their attractive leaves. For, as most people discover,
fresh herbs offer an endless source of inspiration to the creative cook.

PREVIOUS PAGE *left to right* ROSEMARY KEBABS OF CHAR-GRILLED SUMMER VEGETABLES, *page* 51;

AUTUMN SALAD, *page* 51; SUMMER SALAD, *page* 51.

ROSEMARY KEBABS OF CHAR-GRILLED SUMMER VEGETABLES

The slightly woody stems of the rosemary bush make admirable herbal skewers for vegetables, fruit, fish and meat. Grill the vegetables over charcoal for a superb flavour and serve with a spiced rosemary dressing and plenty of freshly baked bread.

SERVES 4–6

**a selection of summer vegetables suitable for grilling, such as courgettes, sweet peppers, tomatoes, mushrooms, whole cloves of garlic, red onions
8–12 stiff stems of rosemary with most of the leaves removed or, alternatively, wooden skewers**

MARINATING DRESSING

**2 tablespoons lemon and garlic vinegar (see page 79)
1 tablespoon water
3 star anise
6 green peppercorns, coarsely ground
1 tablespoon fresh rosemary leaves
150ml (¼ pint) mild olive oil or sunflower oil**

Make the dressing by gently heating the vinegar and water with the star anise, peppercorns and rosemary leaves in a small pan. Bring almost to the boil, then remove from the heat and allow to cool slightly before mixing in the sunflower or olive oil.

Prepare the vegetables by washing and trimming where necessary. Cut the vegetables into similar size pieces, large enough to be threaded on to the skewers. Place the vegetables in a dish, pour over the dressing and toss the ingredients gently together. Leave to marinate for at least 1–2 hours until you are ready to cook.

Thread the vegetables on to the rosemary stems or skewers, alternating the different kinds to create an interesting mixture of colours and textures. Cook over a moderately hot charcoal grill, turning as required, until the vegetables are cooked. Serve with the remaining dressing spooned over.

FOUR SEASONS SALADS

Begone dull salad: for as each of the seasons of the year arrives the fortunate herb gardener is able to prepare unusual and delectable salads that reflect the kaleidoscope of different leaves and flowers harvested from his plants. So that, for example, a spring salad is based on the fresh green and yellow shades of new growth while an autumn salad glows with the claret and burgundy tones of the end of summer. When concocting your own salads, look for colour and flavour harmonies in the leaves and blooms so that each salad has a distinctive character.

A SPRING SALAD

The predominant colours in this salad are green and cream. Arrange the leaves attractively on individual plates and hand the dressing separately. For each person select a handful of tender young leaves from the following: sorrel, both French and Buckler, young spinach leaves, lamb's lettuce or mâche, cooked asparagus tips, blanched baby mangetout peas, sprigs of variegated ginger mint, dill shoots, sprigs of sweet cicely, and the creamy heads of sweet cicely and elderflowers – separated into their separate blooms. For a spring salad dressing; mix together for each person 1 tablespoon hazelnut oil, 1 tablespoon safflower oil and 1 teaspoon dill-flavoured vinegar (see page 79). Season to taste with salt and pepper. Dribble the dressing over the salads and each person can gently toss the leaves to coat them evenly just before eating.

A SUMMER SALAD

A cheerful orange and yellow salad. Arrange each serving of salad with some of the following: bronze-leaved oak-leaf lettuce, fresh coriander leaves, nasturtium leaves – especially the yellow-veined Atlantic varieties, narrow strips of roasted green, red and yellow peppers, red and yellow nasturtium flowers, marigold petals, small sprigs of basil and mint, long thinly shredded zest of lemon. To dress each salad, mix 2 tablespoons garlic olive oil

(see page 86) with 1–2 teaspoons nasturtium and lemon vinegar (see page 79), some finely chopped basil or flat-leaf parsley, according to their availability, and seasoning of salt and freshly milled pepper to taste.

AN AUTUMN SALAD

The russet, red and purple colours of autumn fruits are the key to this salad. Assemble a background to the salad using red radicchio leaves, purple-flushed Continuity or Four Seasons lettuce, perella leaves and red mountain spinach or orache, and garnish with halved and seeded dark red grapes, black olives, sprigs of pink thyme flowers, a few sprigs of bronze fennel and tiny young leaves of red sage. Complete with a few purple hearts-ease pansies (or Johnny jump ups) and some needles of purple chive flowers. Make the dressing for each salad by mixing 1 teaspoon prepared tapenade with 2 tablespoons walnut oil and some hyssop vinegar (see page 79) and season to taste.

A WINTER SALAD

In this pale green, yellow and ochre-coloured salad, several of the ingredients are blanched by covering the plants with an upturned box to exclude the light for 1–2 weeks. This gives a normally bitter-tasting salad plant an agreeable nutty flavour which is most appetizing during the short days of winter. Select the ingredients for the salad from the following: endive frisée, blanched dandelion leaves, blanched escarole or Batavian endive, yellow chives produced by excluding the light from chive shoots for 7– 10 days, a few yellow bean sprouts, and spring onions that have been trimmed, shredded lengthways and soaked in iced water for 1 hour. The salad is garnished at the last moment with whole roasted cloves of garlic and garlic croûtons.

For the dressing for each salad, blend 2 tablespoons of olive oil from roasting the garlic cloves with 1–2 teaspoons of thyme vinegar (see page 79) and seasoning of salt and freshly milled pepper to taste. Dress the salad just before serving.

GRILLED BABY LEEKS

Steamed baby leeks grilled with citrus butter make an excellent hot salad or side dish.

SERVES 3–4
225–340g (8–12oz) baby leeks, trimmed
and washed
a handful of bay leaves
60g (2oz) butter
½ teaspoon finely grated lime or orange
zest

Steam the baby leeks over a layer of bay leaves in a steaming basket for 5–10 minutes until tender. Arrange the leeks in a single layer on a heat-proof dish.

Melt the butter with the lime or orange zest and brush over the leeks. Place under a very hot grill for 3–5 minutes until starting to brown. Remove from the grill and serve the leeks hot or warm with the citrus butter spooned over them.

ONION AND LEMON THYME TART

The combination of crisp thyme-flavoured pastry and rich creamy onion filling is very good indeed. Serve the tart straight from the oven while piping hot.

SERVES 6
PASTRY
120g (4oz) plain flour
½ teaspoon lemon thyme leaves, chopped
60g (2oz) butter, softened
2 egg yolks
1 egg white
FILLING
30g (1oz) butter
120g (4oz) peeled, chopped onion
2 tablespoons milk
2 spring onions, chopped
3 eggs
150ml (¼ pint) double cream
a pinch of grated nutmeg
salt
6 small sprigs of lemon thyme

First make the pastry: sift the flour into a bowl and stir in the chopped thyme. Add the butter and egg yolks and rub together until the mixture forms a soft dough. Form into a ball, wrap and chill for 30 minutes.

Roll out the pastry and use to line a buttered 23cm (9in) fluted flan tin. Brush the pastry case with the lightly whisked egg white and prick all over with a fork. Bake in a moderately hot oven (200°C, 400°F, gas mark 6) for 10 minutes or until the pastry is set. Remove from the oven and set aside until needed. (If need be, the pastry case can be made ahead and frozen until required. Simply thaw the pastry at room temperature for 1 hour before adding the filling.)

Melt the butter in a saucepan and stir in the chopped onion. Cook, stirring now and again, for 4–5 minutes without allowing the butter to brown. Add the milk, cover and cook over medium-low heat for 8–12 minutes or until the onion is cooked.

Remove the pan from the heat and stir in the spring onions. Cool slightly, then mix in the eggs lightly beaten with the cream, nutmeg and a little salt. Pour this filling into the pastry case and bake at the same temperature for 20–25 minutes or until set.

Remove from the oven, garnish with the sprigs of lemon thyme and serve straight away, before the tart begins to cool.

POTATO PIE WITH GARLIC AND PARSLEY

This classic dish of the French country kitchen retains its deserved popularity despite every twist of gastronomic fashion.

SERVES 6
450g (1lb) peeled waxy potatoes such as
Desiree
2 cloves garlic, finely chopped
2–3 tablespoons chopped flat-leaf parsley
salt and freshly milled black pepper
340g (12oz) puff pastry
1 large egg, beaten
100ml (3½fl oz) crème fraîche or double
cream

Slice the potatoes very thinly into a bowl and mix with the garlic, parsley and some salt and freshly milled black pepper.

Roll out just over half the pastry and use to line a 20cm (8in) diameter tart or quiche tin. Layer the seasoned potato slices in the pastry case and cover with the rest of the pastry rolled to fit. Brush the top of the pie with beaten egg, then use a sharp-bladed knife to mark a criss-cross pattern on top. Cut a steam vent in the pastry lid and position a roll of foil or baking paper in the vent to prevent it closing.

Bake the pie in a moderately hot oven (200°C, 400°F, gas mark 6) for 50 minutes.

Remove the pie from the oven. Mix the remaining egg with the crème fraîche and pour into the steam vent. Bake the pie for a further 8–12 minutes, then serve immediately, cut into wedges.

This lovely layered pie (right) is a subtle variation on the tradition of serving the parsley herb with potatoes. It is one of the tastiest ways of serving potatoes.

ARMENIAN OKRA SALAD

Okra, or ladies' fingers, cooked with tomatoes makes its own colourful and delicious sauce. Serve the salad as a separate first course or use to accompany cold ham or poultry as a main course for a summer lunch.

SERVES 6–8
450g (1lb) okra
2 tablespoons sunflower oil
1 medium onion, finely chopped
450g (1lb) tomatoes, peeled and roughly chopped
1 teaspoon sugar
salt and freshly milled black pepper
150ml (¼ pint) Greek style goats' or sheeps' milk yoghurt
2–3 tablespoons finely chopped mint
a squeeze of lemon juice

Trim the stalk end of each okra and rinse them in cold water, then drain well.

Heat the oil in a large shallow pan and soften the onion over moderate heat for 5 minutes until golden and translucent. Add the tomatoes, sugar, salt and pepper and cook, stirring, for 4 minutes.

Add the okra and spoon the tomato mixture over them. Cook the mixture over moderate heat for 20–30 minutes, turning over the okra now and again, until well cooked, by which time the tomatoes and onion should have cooked down enough to make a rich red sauce for the okra.

Spoon the mixture on to a shallow dish or plate and allow to cool. Mix the yoghurt with the mint and add lemon juice to taste. As a finishing touch, lightly spoon the yoghurt mixture over the okra and set aside until ready to serve.

BLANCHED VEGETABLE SALAD WITH FRANKFURT GREEN SAUCE

This delicious salad of dressed blanched vegetables looks most attractive when arranged in diagonal rows. The recipe for the famous Green Sauce from Frankfurt, which she describes as 'nice and easy', came from my dear friend Christel Scholpp.

SERVES 6–8
900g-1.4kg (2–3lb) mixed raw vegetables, such as mangetout peas, cauliflower florets, broccoli florets, baby carrots, radishes, baby turnips, baby sweetcorn, French beans, baby courgettes, etc.
salt
a bouquet garni of fresh herbs (see page 87)
120g (4oz) red and/or yellow cherry tomatoes
sprigs of fresh herbs, to garnish (optional)
DRESSING
6 tablespoons herb-flavoured oil (see page 86)
1 tablespoon lemon and garlic vinegar (see page 79)
GREEN SAUCE
6 tablespoons finely chopped fresh herbs, including some or all of the following: sorrel, salad burnet, borage, dill, parsley, chives, chervil, tarragon and lovage
3 hard-boiled eggs, shelled and roughly chopped
150ml (¼ pint) sunflower or olive oil, plain or herb-flavoured
about 2 tablespoons tarragon or dill vinegar
salt and freshly milled pepper
caster sugar
made mustard

Wash and trim the vegetables where necessary. Blanch each vegetable separately until almost cooked either by steaming or in a pan of boiling salted water containing a bouquet garni. Drain the vegetables and place in a large bowl. Add herb oil and vinegar and toss gently until lightly coated with the dressing.

Peel the tomatoes by dipping them briefly in boiling water and then in cold water before removing the skins. Spoon some of the oil and vinegar dressing from the vegetables over them and arrange the tomatoes in a neat row, stalk side down, diagonally across the middle of a serving dish. Arrange the rest of the vegetables in rows next to the tomatoes, varying the colours and shapes to make an attractive presentation. If you wish, garnish the dish by placing sprigs of herbs around the rim in a fresh leafy border.

To make the sauce, mix the herbs with the eggs in a food processor to a fairly smooth paste. Alternatively, press the mixture through a fine sieve. Gradually beat in the oil, drop by drop as when making mayonnaise. Mix in vinegar, seasoning, sugar and mustard to taste.

Spoon the sauce into a wooden or pottery bowl and serve with the vegetable salad.

MARINATED SHIITAKE MUSHROOMS

A cold mushroom salad, flavoured with garlic and coriander leaves, this American recipe was inspired by the cooking of Greens, San Francisco's pre-eminent vegetarian restaurant.

SERVES 4
225g (8oz) fresh shiitake mushrooms
2–3 tablespoons olive oil
a few drops of sesame oil
1 clove garlic, halved
2–3 tablespoons Californian chardonnay or lime juice
1 tablespoon coriander, roughly chopped leaves
salt and freshly milled black pepper
a little extra olive oil

Trim a sliver from the stalk end of each mushroom and wipe over with a damp cloth. Heat the olive and sesame oils in a large shallow pan and stir in the garlic. Cook for a short while but do not let the garlic colour.

Add the mushrooms and turn them over in the oil, then cover the pan and cook over a low heat for about 5–10 minutes until they are cooked through.

Transfer the mushrooms to a shallow dish and, if you wish, discard the garlic. Add the white wine or lime juice to the pan and boil the liquid fast for 2–3 minutes until syrupy. Remove from the heat and gradually stir in the coriander leaves, seasoning and additional olive oil. Spoon the mixture over the cooked mushrooms.

Set aside in a cold place to marinate for 2–3 hours, then serve with some sourdough or French bread.

ASPARAGUS WITH LEMON AND TARRAGON MOUSSELINE SAUCE

The asparagus season arrives with the first tender young shoots of tarragon. The combination of the two exquisite flavours is a timeless example of French country cooking.

SERVES 4
700–900g (1½–2lb) fresh asparagus,
preferably a green variety
bay leaves and sprigs of tarragon, to
steam (optional)
SAUCE MOUSSELINE
3 egg yolks
1 tablespoon tarragon vinegar
salt
2–3 green peppercorns, finely crushed
225g (8oz) unsalted butter, creamed with
1 teaspoon finely chopped tarragon
¼ teaspoon finely grated lemon zest
juice of ½–1 lemon
100ml (3½fl oz) crème fraîche

Trim the cut end of each asparagus spear, then tie them in one or several bundles with a length of cotton tape.

Cook the asparagus in 5–7.5cm (2–3in) of lightly salted boiling water, with the cut ends standing in the water and the tips covered with a hood of foil that you tuck inside the pan so that the tips cook in the steam. Alternatively, steam the asparagus in a Chinese steaming basket lined with bay leaves and sprigs of tarragon. Freshly cut asparagus takes 6–12

minutes to cook depending on its size; bought asparagus usually takes a little longer. The asparagus is cooked when the point of a sharp knife goes easily into the cut end of the spear. When cooked, drain the asparagus, arrange on a warm serving dish and keep warm by covering with a clean dry cloth.

To make the sauce, whisk the egg yolks with the vinegar, a little salt and the green pepper-corns in a bowl placed over a pan of hot water. Add the butter in small lumps, whisking in each addition. The butter should soften but not melt. If the bowl gets too hot, immediately stand it in a bowl of ice-cold water to cool and then replace it over the hot water. Continue whisking the butter into the sauce, which should mount and thicken like a mayonnaise.

Remove the bowl from the heat and gradually whisk in sufficient lemon juice and the lemon zest to sharpen the flavour agreeably. Fold in the cream, check the seasoning and serve in a bowl with the asparagus.

BAKED SWEET POTATOES WITH CHIVE AND GINGER BUTTER

Two varieties of sweet potatoes are generally available in Europe, both are delicious.

SERVES 4
4 medium-sized sweet potatoes
120g (4oz) butter, softened
a walnut-size piece of fresh root ginger,
peeled and finely grated
2 tablespoons finely chopped chives
salt and freshly milled pepper
a squeeze of lemon juice

Scrub the sweet potatoes, prick their skins and place on a lightly oiled baking sheet. Bake in a moderately hot oven (190°C, 375°F, gas mark 5) for 40–60 minutes, or until cooked.

Meanwhile, cream the butter with the grated ginger and the chopped chives. Season to taste with salt, pepper and lemon juice.

Halve the potatoes lengthways and arrange on a cloth-lined dish or wooden bowl. Serve straight away with the savoury butter.

DESSERTS AND PUDDINGS

During long winter hours of armchair gardening I sometimes plan a confectionery
border as a kind of annexe to my herb garden. In it I'd grow all the herbs
whose leaves, flowers and seeds are a delight when used in sweet dishes and desserts.
These are the highly perfumed herbs whose scent amplifies the flavours of
a dish in a most bewitching fashion: the flowers and leaves of lavender and
lemon verbena, pineapple sage and angelica, eau-de-cologne *and*
ginger mint, sweet cicely and bergamot. And to these one must add the most
ancient of herbal delights, the rose, the sweet violet and the muscat-scented elderflower.
This chorus of scent would need to be planted near the house,
under a window perhaps, where the perfume could waft indoors.
The most ephemeral plants in the sweet herb border are the edible flowers;
marigolds, nasturtiums and heart's-ease pansies, gilly-flowers and cottage pinks.
Some of the most charming recipes for using these plants come from
the sixteenth and seventeenth centuries. Small wonder that the sugared flowers
and perfumed preserves that were the products of the still rooms of
Elizabethan houses are no less appealing to the herb gardening cooks of today.
Milk, cream, honey and sugar all readily absorb the volatile oils from aromatic
herbs when gently heated. Simply add the herbs to the liquid
in a heavy-based pan or a bain-marie *and stir over moderate heat until the*
mixture is subtly scented. Strain the mixture, discard the herbs
and you have a perfumed preparation for making custards, sorbets and syllabubs.

PREVIOUS PAGE *left to right* JASMINE TEA CREAM, *page* 65;
NECTARINE AND LEMON VERBENA ICE CREAM, *page* 61;
STUFFED PEACHES WITH PEACH LEAF CUSTARD, *page* 66.

NECTARINE AND LEMON VERBENA ICE CREAM IN ROSE CHOCOLATE CASES

For my daughter's birthday in mid-August I usually devise a new ice cream. This blend of crushed ripe nectarines scented with lemon verbena was especially good. The unusual rose water and chocolate cases work particularly well filled with summer fruit ice-cream.

SERVES 12
6 leaves of lemon verbena
60ml (2fl oz) muscat de Rivesaltes or other sweet white wine
8 ripe nectarines
90–120g (3–4oz) caster sugar
450ml (¾ pint) double cream
2 egg whites
ROSE CHOCOLATE CASES
225g (8oz) plain dessert chocolate, broken into pieces
2 tablespoons double cream
1 teaspoon rose water
12 paper cake cases
12 rose leaves

Chop the leaves of lemon verbena and infuse in the wine over low heat for 3 minutes. Remove from the heat and set aside.

Wash and dry the nectarines and slice the fruit into a food processor, discarding the stones. Purée the fruit with the wine and lemon verbena mixture. Stir in the sugar.

Whisk the cream until thick but still glossy and fold in the nectarine mixture. Whisk the egg whites until stiff and fold into the mixture. Freeze in an electric sorbetière or pour the mixture into a lidded plastic box and still-freeze until almost firm.

To make the chocolate cases, melt the chocolate gently in a pan with the cream. Remove from the heat and stir in the rose water. Place the paper cases in a patty tin and spoon melted chocolate into each one, spreading a thin layer over the bottom and sides of each case. Place the patty tin in the freezer until the chocolate is set. Spoon the remaining chocolate over the underside of each rose leaf and chill until set.

Peel the paper layer from the chocolate cases and the rose leaves from the chocolate leaves, and replace the chocolate cases and leaves in the freezer until you are ready to serve the ice cream.

Spoon ice cream into each chocolate case and decorate with a chocolate leaf. Place the filled cases on a dish and scatter a few fresh rose petals around them.

MUSCAT GRAPE AND ELDERFLOWER TART

The deliciously similar flavours of elderflower and muscat grapes are well exploited in this lovely tart which makes a perfect end to a summer meal.

SERVES 6–8
120g (4oz) sugar
150ml (¼ pint) cold water
3 heads of elderflower
1–2 tablespoons Beaumes de Venise muscat wine
450g (1lb) red or white seedless muscat grapes
90g (3oz) cream cheese
150ml (¼ pint) soured cream
a 23cm (9in) baked pastry tart case

In a medium size pan, dissolve the sugar in the water and bring to the boil. Simmer for 4 minutes, then remove from the heat and cool slightly. Add the elderflower to the syrup and leave to infuse for 3–4 minutes, then discard the heads of the flower.

Stir one or two tablespoons of the Beaumes de Venise muscat wine into the syrup, according to taste, and add the red or white seedless grapes, which you should have already washed and halved. Set aside in a cool place to macerate until ready to fill the tart.

Blend the cream cheese with the soured cream and sweeten to taste with some of the elderflower syrup. Spoon the cream into the pastry case and spread evenly. Arrange the halved grapes in circles on top and spoon a little of the syrup over them. Set aside for no more than 2 hours before serving.

ROSE-PETAL SORBET WITH ROSE-PETAL MERINGUES

This is the kind of charming and romantic dish that I make in a small quantity for a birthday lunch with my daughter or a special friend. Serve the pale pink confection in a fine stemmed glass so that the delicate colour can be appreciated.

SERVES 4
225g (8oz) caster sugar
450ml (¾ pint) cold water
600ml (1 pint) red or pink scented rose petals
a squeeze of lemon juice
rose petals, fresh or crystallized, to serve
MERINGUES
2 egg whites
120g (4oz) rose-scented sugar (see page 89)
1–2 drops of pink food colouring
a little extra caster sugar

Dissolve the sugar in the water over medium heat. Bring to the boil and simmer for 5 minutes. Remove the pan from the heat and stir in the rose petals. Set aside for 2 hours until the syrup has absorbed most of the fragrance.

Strain the syrup into a bowl and add a squeeze of lemon juice to adjust the flavour. Freeze in an electric sorbetière, or still-freeze in the freezer, whisking the mixture every half hour to make a smoother sorbet. Store the sorbet in the freezer until needed.

To make the meringues, whisk the egg whites until stiff, then whisk in half the sugar. Gently fold in the rest of the sugar and, if desired, tint the mixture a very pale pink with food colouring. Spoon or pipe teaspoons of the mixture on to sheets of baking parchment on baking trays. Sprinkle with a little extra sugar to give the meringues a frosted finish.

Bake in a cool oven (100°C, 200°F, gas mark ¼) for 1½–2 hours. Turn off the oven and leave the meringues inside for 3 hours until cold. Carefully remove from the baking paper.

Serve the sorbet in pretty glass dishes accompanied by the meringues.

QUINCE AND APPLE CUSTARD TART WITH SWEET CICELY CREAM

The scented quince effectively perfumes its fellow ingredients with the result that an apple or a pear tart made with an almond pastry reflects a glorious marriage of flavours.

SERVES 6–8
ALMOND PASTRY
120g (4oz) plain flour
60g (2oz) ground almonds
30g (1oz) icing sugar
90g (3oz) butter
2–3 tablespoons milk
FILLING
45g (1½oz) amaretti or almond macaroon crumbs
450g (1lb) ripe Cox's Orange Pippin apples
1 large ripe quince, peeled, sliced and cooked
150ml (¼ pint) double cream
90g (3oz) vanilla-flavoured sugar
2 eggs
SWEET CICELY CREAM
3 leaves of sweet cicely
2 tablespoons muscat or sweet white wine such as a montbazillac
1–2 tablespoons sugar
300ml (½ pint) whipping cream
a few small leaves and flowers of sweet cicely, to decorate

To make the pastry, sift the flour, almonds and sugar into a bowl. Rub in butter and add milk to mix to a dough. Form the dough into a ball, wrap and refrigerate for 30 minutes.

Meanwhile, make the sweet cicely cream. Infuse the 3 leaves in the wine in a small pan over low heat for 5 minutes. Strain into a bowl and stir in the sugar. When cool, add the cream and whip until thick. Spoon into a pretty bowl and decorate with small sprigs and flowers of sweet cicely. Keep in a cool place.

Roll out the dough and use to line a 23cm (9in) pie dish about 5cm (2in) deep. Crimp the edges of the pastry case and spread the amaretti crumbs over the bottom.

Peel, core and slice the apples and arrange in the pastry case with the sliced quince. Lightly whisk the cream with the sugar and eggs and pour over the fruit. Bake in a moderately hot oven (200°C, 400°F, gas mark 6) for 20 minutes, then lower the heat to moderate (180°C, 350°F, gas mark 4) and bake for a further 10–15 minutes until the apples are tender and the custard is set. Remove from the oven and serve warm or cold.

ELDERFLOWER SYLLABUB

This is one of those light-as-air puddings that make the perfect end to a summer meal. A traditional syllabub was made by milking the cow straight into the wine or fruit syrup.

SERVES 4
75g (2½oz) caster sugar
5 tablespoons cold water
3 heads of elderflower
1 tablespoon sweet white wine
300ml (½ pint) double cream
1 egg white
small sprigs of elderflower, candied violets or primroses to decorate

Dissolve the sugar in the water over medium heat. Bring to the boil and simmer for 3 minutes. Remove the syrup from the heat and cool for 2 minutes, then add the elderflower heads and infuse for 2–3 minutes. Strain the syrup into a bowl and stir in the sweet white wine. Cool the syrup.

Place 1 teaspoon of the syrup in the bottom of each of 4 stemmed glasses. Mix the remaining syrup with the cream and whip until stiff but still glossy. Whisk the egg white until stiff and fold into the cream.

Spoon the mixture into the glasses and chill for at least 30 minutes. Decorate the syllabub with elderflower, candied violets or primroses just before serving.

The delicate flavours of elderflower and sweet cicely impart a subtle flavour and a summertime aroma to these dishes.

EXOTIC FRUIT AND FLOWER SALAD IN AN ICE-BOWL

If you have both passion fruit and passion flowers available, then it's a pretty idea to freeze the flowers – which, by the way, are not edible – in the ice-bowl and add the passion fruit to the salad. However, any pretty flowers can be included in the bowl. For a comprehensive list of edible flowers see page 88.

SERVES 6–10
2 handfuls of pretty flowers and petals
such as pinks, pansies, borage flowers
and rose petals
SALAD
1 ripe Charentais or Galia melon
1 mango
8–12 fresh lychees
1 carambola (star fruit)
1 pawpaw
4 passion fruit
caster sugar or clear honey to taste
a few drops of orange-flower water
edible flowers, to decorate

The ice-bowl can be made several days ahead and stored in the freezer until needed. Half fill a large shallow bowl with cold water. Trim the stems from the flowers and add to the water. Place the bowl on a firm level base in the freezer and leave for 1–2 hours until the water is starting to freeze around the edges. Now place a second, slightly smaller bowl inside the first bowl. Add a small weight to make the bowl float at the right depth and place corks or crumpled foil around the edge to locate the second bowl centrally. Add a few more flowers to the water and freeze until the water has turned to ice.

Remove from the freezer and carefully pour warm water into the smaller bowl to melt the

This exotic fruit and flower salad in an ice-bowl never fails to create a dramatic impression at the dinner table and can easily be made in advance. Borage flowers are here enhanced by the addition of vibrantly-coloured passion flowers.

ice just enough to help you remove the bowl. Turn the ice-bowl upside down and pour warm water over the larger bowl so you can lift it off. Wrap the ice-bowl in freezer film and store carefully in the freezer until needed.

To make the fruit and flower salad, peel and deseed the fruit as required and cut into bite-size pieces. Gently toss together in a mixing bowl with the flesh from the passion fruit. If desired, add a little sugar or honey to sweeten, and flavour with orange flower water. Chill the fruit salad until ready to serve.

Place the ice-bowl on a folded napkin on a platter and fill with the fruit salad. Decorate with the extra edible flowers that you have left over and serve straight away.

JASMINE TEA CREAM

Jasmine tea is a large-leaf black China tea scented with the dried flowers of the highly perfumed white jasmine. This delicately flavoured light cream looks charming decorated with fresh jasmine blooms.

SERVES 6
2 tablespoons jasmine tea leaves
150ml ($\frac{1}{4}$ pint) boiling water
60g (2oz) caster sugar
300ml ($\frac{1}{2}$ pint) single cream
2 tablespoons powdered gelatine
2 tablespoons cold water
fresh jasmine flowers, to decorate

Measure the tea in a warmed saucepan, pour over the boiling water and leave to infuse for 1 minute. Add the sugar and cream and slowly bring the mixture to the boil over gentle heat, stirring all the time. Check the taste every so often until the cream is well-flavoured.

Remove from the heat and strain the cream into a bowl. Soften the gelatine in the cold water and heat gently until dissolved. Cool slightly, then pour in a fine stream into the cream, stirring all the time.

Pour the cream into a pretty glass bowl or several small dishes and put aside in a cold place until lightly set. Decorate the tea cream with jasmine blossoms just before serving.

SPRINGTIME ANGEL CAKE WITH SUGARED FLOWERS

This very light white cake, smothered in whipped cream and decorated with sugared spring flowers is pretty enough to serve at Easter or for an anniversary.

SERVES 8–10
75g (3oz) plain flour
15g ($\frac{1}{2}$oz) cornflour
175g (6oz) caster sugar
6 size-2 egg whites
1 teaspoon cream of tartar
$\frac{1}{2}$ teaspoon vanilla essence
$\frac{1}{4}$ teaspoon almond essence
ALMOND CREAM
300ml ($\frac{1}{2}$ pint) whipping cream
60g (2oz) vanilla-flavoured sugar
a few drops of almond essence
1–2 teaspoons peach brandy
SUGARED FLOWERS
1 egg white
caster sugar
fresh violets and primroses

Sift the flour with the cornflour and 120g (4oz) of the caster sugar on to a piece of greaseproof paper. Whisk the egg whites with the cream of tartar in a wide bowl until stiff and fluffy but still a little moist (do not whisk until dry). Sprinkle the remaining sugar over the egg whites and gently whisk in. Fold in the vanilla and almond essences. Sift some of the flour mixture over the egg whites and gradually fold it in. Repeat with the remaining flour mixture. Spoon the mixture into an ungreased non-stick 25cm (10in) ring tin and smooth level.

Bake in a moderate oven (170°C, 325°F, gas mark 3) for 45–55 minutes until the cake is cooked. It will shrink away from the tin slightly when it is ready. Cool in the tin for 5 minutes, then turn the cake out on to a wire rack.

Prepare the sugared flowers (see page 88).

To make the almond cream, whip the cream with the vanilla-flavoured sugar until thick and smooth. Flavour to taste with the almond essence and peach brandy.

Spread the cream all over the cake and decorate with the sugared flowers.

STUFFED PEACHES WITH PEACH LEAF CUSTARD

This Italian pudding of peaches stuffed with amaretti biscuits is a real delight served with smooth custard flavoured with peach leaves.

SERVES 8
8 large, ripe peaches
60g (2oz) amaretti biscuits, crushed
60g (2oz) ground almonds
1 tablespoon Amaretti di Sarone liqueur
finely grated zest and juice of 1 orange
300ml (½ pint) medium dry Italian white wine
1–2 tablespoons caster sugar
CUSTARD
600ml (1 pint) single cream
8 egg yolks
60g (2oz) vanilla-flavoured caster sugar
8 tender young peach leaves

First make the custard. Heat the cream in a double boiler. Whisk the egg yolks with the sugar in a bowl. When the cream is almost boiling, whisk into the egg yolks, then return to the pan and add the peach leaves.

Cook, stirring all the time, for 5–8 minutes until the custard thickens sufficiently to coat the back of the spoon. Do not allow the custard to boil or the eggs will separate and spoil the smoothness. Strain the custard into a pretty glass dish or jug and leave until cool.

Cover one or two peaches at a time with boiling water and leave for 1–2 minutes, then cool in cold water and carefully remove the skins. Halve and stone the fruit.

Mix the biscuit crumbs with the ground almonds, liqueur and orange zest and add sufficient juice to bind the mixture together. Divide the mixture between the peaches, sandwiching it between the two halves.

Place the peaches in a flameproof dish and pour the wine over them. Bake in a moderate oven (180°C, 350°F, gas mark 4) for 15–20 minutes until tender. Remove from the oven and sprinkle caster sugar over each peach. Place under a very hot grill until the sugar has caramelized to a golden brown. Serve warm or cold with the peach leaf custard.

BANANA, LIME AND PINEAPPLE SAGE YOGHURT ICE

The leaves of pineapple sage have a strong pineapple scent and flavour which acts as a delightful foil to the sweetness of bananas.

SERVES 8
900g (2lb) ripe bananas
finely grated zest and juice of 1 lime
120g (4oz) caster sugar
300ml (½ pint) low-fat natural yoghurt
6 leaves of pineapple sage, chopped
2 egg whites
a small handful of pineapple sage flowers, to decorate

Peel the bananas and mash until smooth with the lime zest and juice. Stir in the sugar, yoghurt and chopped pineapple sage until well combined. Whisk the egg whites until stiff and fold into the mixture.

Freeze the mixture in an electric sorbetière or in a lidded plastic box and still-freeze until firm. Serve in coupé dishes, decorated with the scarlet flowers of pineapple sage.
Note: as an alternative to pineapple sage, try pineapple-scented geranium leaves.

MINTED PEARS ON CHOCOLATE SHORTBREAD

The crisp chocolate shortbread can be made ahead and stored in the freezer or refrigerator until needed.

SERVES 6
3 almost ripe dessert pears
60g (2oz) caster sugar
150ml (¼ pint) water
2 sprigs of mint
a small strip of lemon peel
85g (3oz) cream cheese
1–2 teaspoons caster sugar
1–2 teaspoons Poire William liqueur
6 sprigs of frosted mint leaves, to decorate (see page 88)
CHOCOLATE SHORTBREAD
140g (5oz) plain flour
15g (½oz) cocoa powder
a pinch of ground cinnamon
120g (4oz) butter, softened
70g (2½oz) vanilla-flavoured caster sugar

Peel, halve and core the pears. Dissolve the sugar in the water and bring to the boil. Add the mint and lemon peel and simmer for 3 minutes. Add the halved pears and poach gently for 8–12 minutes until almost cooked.

Remove from the heat, cover the pan and leave for 10–15 minutes to complete the cooking. Then use a slotted spoon to transfer the pears to a plate. Discard the mint and the lemon peel and boil the syrup until reduced to 2–3 tablespoons. Set aside to cool.

To make the shortbread, sift the flour, cocoa and cinnamon into a bowl. Cream the butter with the sugar until fluffy, then gradually work in the flour mixture until you can form the dough into a ball.

Place a sheet of baking parchment on a baking tray and pat or roll out the dough on it to make a round 20cm (8in) in diameter. Pinch the edge into a fluted shape and prick all over with the prongs of a fork. Bake in a moderate oven (180°C, 350°F, gas mark 4) for 25–30 minutes. Cool on the baking tray for 5 minutes, then transfer to a wire rack or flat serving plate.

Blend the cream cheese with the sugar and flavour with the liqueur. Spread the mixture over the shortbread base. Arrange the pears on top, either whole or sliced, pointing to the centre. Spoon over the pear syrup and garnish with sprigs of frosted mint leaves. This dessert is best served within 2 hours while the shortbread is still crisp.

Pears, mint and chocolate shortbread make a subtle and tangy dessert which is a welcome change from the classic dish of pears in red wine. Other fruit desserts with herbs include Nectarine and Lemon Verbena Ice Cream (see page 61) and Quince and Apple Custard Tart with Sweet Cicely Cream (see page 62).

BREADS, CAKES AND BISCUITS

*In classical Rome, bakers used to place a seedhead of fennel under their loaves as
they slid them into the oven. Chinese cooks have added poppy seeds
to their steamed buns for centuries and today, in Devon and Cornwall, a golden
saffron doughcake studded with dried fruit, a relic of medieval times, is still baked.
After many years of home-baking, my own favourite biscuit remains
a thin pale disc of buttery shortbread flecked and flavoured with
finely chopped leaves of rosemary or lavender.
How beautifully an aromatic herb pervades a pastry or dough during baking.
A few leaves of rose-scented geranium placed in a cake tin,
under the mixture, perfumes a whole cake by the time it is taken from the oven.
Edible herb flowers add a new and unexpected dimension to the tea table:
marigold sandwiches or thinly sliced brioche enclosing sugared rose petals or a
lavender honey wafer are best accompanied by a herb tisane or tea,
ideally prepared with a sprig of fresh rosemary, a handful of lime flowers or some
leaves of lemon balm. Increasingly, people young and old are finding that
herbal tea makes a stimulating yet relaxing drink with none of the disadvantages
of caffeine, while a tisane's digestive properties only adds to its charm.
But baking with herbs is not restricted to sweet dishes.
Timeless baking traditions have produced classic breads that are characterized
by their appropriate herbs. The flat sage breads of Italy,
the thyme-flavoured* fougasse *of Provence and the English plaited loaf
infused with marjoram – once specially made to celebrate the harvest
– are all enduring yeast-leavened loaves.*

PREVIOUS PAGE CROISSANTS FILLED WITH BRAISED STRAWBERRIES

AND LAVENDER HONEY, *page 71.*

HERB BUTTERS

Butter is one of the most delicious vehicles for the aromatic essential oils in herbs. And there are very few dishes, such as soups and sauces, freshly cooked vegetables or a warm loaf of bread, that are not improved with a pat of a well-flavoured herb butter. The simplest herb butter is no more than a blend of freshly chopped herbs and a sweet unsalted butter. The result stores well in the refrigerator for 2–3 weeks and in the freezer for 2–3 months.

CHIVE AND LEMON BUTTER: blend 120g (4oz) softened butter with the finely grated zest of ¼ lemon, 1 tablespoon finely chopped chives and lemon juice to taste.

TOMATO AND OREGANO BUTTER: blend 120g (4oz) softened butter with 1 teaspoon tomato paste, ¼ teaspoon finely grated orange zest and 1 teaspoon finely chopped oregano or marjoram.

BLACK OLIVE AND HERBES DE PROVENCE BUTTER: blend 120g (4oz) softened butter with 1–2 tablespoons finely chopped sun-ripened black olives and ½–1 teaspoon crushed *herbes de Provence*, add lemon juice to taste.

DILL BUTTER: blend 120g (4oz) softened butter with 2 hard-boiled egg yolks, 1–2 tablespoons finely chopped dill and lemon juice to taste.

HORSERADISH BUTTER: blend 120g (4oz) softened butter with 2–3 teaspoons finely grated horseradish and lemon juice to taste.

TARTARE BUTTER: blend 120g (4oz) softened butter with ½ teaspoon Dijon mustard, ½ teaspoon Worcestershire sauce, ½ teaspoon lemon juice and 1 teaspoon chopped parsley.

MAITRE D'HOTEL BUTTER: blend 120g (4oz) softened butter with 2 tablespoons finely chopped parsley and 1 tablespoon lemon juice; season to taste with salt and freshly milled pepper.

RAVIGOTE BUTTER: blanch 1 finely chopped shallot and 2–3 tablespoons mixed parsley, chervil, tarragon and chive leaves in boiling water, drain well and chop finely, then blend with 120g (4oz) softened butter and lemon juice to taste.

TARRAGON BUTTER: blend 120g (4oz) softened butter with 2–3 teaspoons finely chopped small tender tarragon leaves and 1–2 teaspoons lemon juice; season to taste with salt and freshly milled pepper.

GARLIC BUTTER: blend 120g (4oz) softened butter with 1–2 crushed cloves garlic, 1 tablespoon finely chopped parsley and a squeeze of lemon juice.

CROISSANTS FILLED WITH BRAISED STRAWBERRIES AND LAVENDER HONEY

One summer morning in France, I decided to make something delicious for breakfast. So I combined ripe strawberries and lavender from the garden with fresh croissants from the village baker. The result tastes wonderful.

SERVES 4
4 large croissants
60g (2oz) butter
340–450g (12–16oz) fresh strawberries, hulled and halved
1–2 tablespoons lavender honey
a few individual lavender flowers or finely chopped lavender leaves
about 150ml (¼ pint) crème fraîche

Heat the croissants in a low oven or under the grill. Meanwhile, melt the butter in a wide, shallow pan and add the strawberries. Cook, stirring, over high heat until they give up their juice. Stir in the honey and cook, stirring, for 3–4 minutes until the juice has thickened into a syrup. Add the lavender flowers or leaves and remove from the heat.

Cut each croissant almost in half, spoon some of the strawberry filling into the centre and add a large spoonful of crème fraîche. Serve immediately.

LAVENDER HONEY WAFERS

These delicate wafer biscuits are excellent eaten quite plain with a sorbet or ice-cream. Or for serving at afternoon tea, the wafers are very good filled with a light rose-water cream and some alpine strawberries.

MAKES ABOUT 24
60g (2oz) unsalted butter, softened
90g (3oz) icing sugar
90g (3oz) plain flour
1 egg white, lightly whisked
4 tablespoons clear lavender honey
120g (4oz) alpine or wood strawberries (if available)
a little extra icing sugar
ROSE WATER CREAM
150ml (¼ pint) whipping cream
rose-scented sugar or plain caster sugar and a few drops of rose-water
1 egg white

Cream the butter with the sifted icing sugar, and gradually mix in the sifted flour with the egg white and honey. Place the mixture in teaspoons on a buttered non-stick baking sheet and spread each spoonful level to make a round 5–7.5cm (2–3in) across. You should be able to make 4–6 lavender honey wafers on each baking sheet.

Bake the wafers in a moderate oven (180°C, 350°F, gas mark 4) for 7–10 minutes until the edges of each wafer are golden brown. Remove from the oven and, as soon as you can handle the wafers, take each one and wrap it loosely around the handle of a wooden spoon so that the wafer has a conical shape. Cool on a wire rack for a few minutes, then carefully remove the wooden handle. When cold, store the wafers in an air-tight plastic box until ready to serve with the cream.

Whip the cream until fairly stiff and sweeten to taste with the rose-scented sugar. Fold in the stiffly whisked egg white.

Spoon some cream into the open end of each wafer and add some alpine strawberries. Dust the wafer lightly with a little icing sugar shaken through a sieve. Serve within 30 minutes, before the wafers soften.

An unusual but inspired selection of ingredients in the form of blackberries and other red fruits are complemented by rose geranium cream which produces a taste of summer right through the year. Remember to freeze some berries each summer to tide you over the winter months. Alternatively, the more common red fruits such as raspberries, strawberries and blackcurrants can be bought frozen at any time of year.

FRESH BLACKBERRY CAKE WITH ROSE GERANIUM CREAM

This summer cake with a centre layer of fresh fruit is just as delicious made with raspberries, bilberries or blackcurrants.

SERVES 8
3 size-2 or 4 size-4 eggs
225g (8oz) plain flour
225g (8oz) rose- or vanilla-flavoured caster sugar (see page 89)
225g (8oz) butter, melted
1 teaspoon rose water (optional)
225g (8oz) fresh, dry blackberries
1 tablespoon caster sugar
1 teaspoon cornflour
$\frac{1}{2}$ teaspoon finely grated orange or lemon zest
ROSE GERANIUM CREAM
3–4 rose geranium leaves
2–3 tablespoons caster sugar
300ml ($\frac{1}{2}$ pint) whipping cream
rose water (optional)
a few small rose geranium leaves, to decorate

Beat the eggs in a bowl and gradually mix in the sifted flour, flavoured sugar, melted butter and rose water. Spoon half the mixture into a greased and lined 23cm (9in) round loose-bottomed cake tin.

Mix the blackberries with the sugar, corn-flour and orange zest and spoon into the tin in an even layer. Carefully spoon the remaining cake mixture over the top and smooth level.

Bake in a moderate oven (180°C, 350°F, gas mark 4) for about 45 minutes until the cake is springy in the middle. Remove from the oven. Cool in the tin for 2 minutes, then transfer to a wire rack.

To make the cream, place the rose ger-anium leaves in a heavy-based pan and add the sugar. Heat gently over a low heat for about 5 minutes, stirring all the time, until the sugar has absorbed some of the aromatic oils of the leaves. Remove from the heat and discard the leaves. Whip the cream with the sugar until stiff and, if you wish, add a little rose water. Spoon the cream into a dish and garnish with small rose geranium leaves.

Serve the cake warm or cold, cut into wedges, with the cream spooned on top.

ANGELICA AND ALMOND CAKE

The green crystallized stem of the angelica plant gives this cake its unusual and attractive flavour. Good quality French angelica can be used but this tends to be rather expensive and not always easy to find, so why not try making your own candied angelica (see page 89).

SERVES 8–12
120g (4oz) butter, softened
120g (4oz) caster sugar
3 eggs
140g (5oz) self-raising flour
60g (2oz) ground almonds
120g (4oz) candied angelica, chopped
60g (2oz) candied orange peel, chopped
MACAROON LAYER
90g (3oz) caster sugar
90g (3oz) ground almonds
30g (1oz) flaked almonds

Cream the butter with the sugar until light and fluffy. Gradually beat in 2 eggs and the yolk of the third. (Set aside the remaining egg white in a bowl.) Sift the flour with the ground almonds and fold into the mixture with the angelica and orange peel.

Spoon the mixture into a greased and lined 18cm (7in) round loose-bottomed cake tin. Lightly whisk the egg white and mix in the sugar and ground almonds. Spread the mixture over the cake and sprinkle the flaked almonds on top.

Bake in a moderate oven (180°C, 350°F, gas mark 4) for 50–60 minutes until the cake is cooked. Halfway through the cooking, place a layer of foil over the cake to prevent the flaked almonds from browning too much. Cool the cake in the tin for 3 minutes, then transfer to a wire rack to cool completely.

This delightful angelica and almond cake is the most delicious treat for a late-summer afternoon tea. Surprisingly light in texture yet full of sweet herbal flavours, it is perhaps best accompanied by a refreshing pot of mild herbal tea.

PLAITED HERB LOAF

Plaited loaves always look appetizing. This milk-bread flavoured with fresh herbs stays fresh for several days if need be.

MAKES 1 LOAF
2 teaspoons dried yeast
150ml (¼ pint) warm water
450g (1lb) unbleached strong white flour
2 teaspoons salt
150ml (¼ pint) warm milk
2 tablespoons herb-flavoured oil
2–3 teaspoons finely chopped fresh herbs:
chives, thyme, rosemary, hyssop,
marjoram
beaten egg or milk
few extra finely chopped herbs

Sprinkle the yeast on to the water in a small bowl and set aside in a warm place for 10 minutes until frothy.

Sift the flour and salt into a mixing bowl and stir in the yeast mixture, milk, oil and chopped herbs. Mix together to make a soft dough. Turn out on to a floured board and knead for 8–10 minutes until the dough feels elastic. Replace the dough in the mixing bowl and place the bowl in a roomy plastic bag. Leave to rise in a warm place for about 1 hour until the dough has doubled in size.

Place the dough on a floured board and knead for 1 minute. Divide the dough into 3 equal pieces. Roll each piece into a sausage about 30cm (12in) long. Press the pieces together at one end and then plait the dough, taking care not to stretch it too much, and press the ends together.

Place the loaf on a greased baking sheet. Brush with beaten egg or milk and sprinkle with the extra herbs. Leave the baking sheet in a warm place for 30–45 minutes until the dough is swollen and puffy.

Bake in a hot oven (220°C, 425°F, gas mark 7) for 30–35 minutes until golden and crusty. Cool on a wire rack.

Herb butters freeze well and for hot dishes they can be used straight from the freezer.

MARIGOLD AND NASTURTIUM LEAF SANDWICHES

During the sixteenth and seventeenth centuries, marigold petals were known as the poor man's saffron. The yellow and orange petals were used to give a saffron colour to butter, cheese and custards. Marigold leaves taste rather like nasturtium leaves with the same slightly peppery flavour. Both marigold and nasturtium leaves can be used as a filling for sandwiches for afternoon tea.

thinly sliced white or brown bread
young marigold and nasturtium leaves
marigold and nasturtium petals and
flowers, to garnish
MARIGOLD BUTTER
120g (4oz) unsalted butter, softened
2 tablespoons marigold petals
a pinch of ground cinnamon
a squeeze of lemon juice

Blend the butter with the marigold petals and cinnamon and add lemon juice to taste.

Spread the marigold butter on to the thinly sliced bread. Cover with a layer of marigold or nasturtium leaves and place a second layer of buttered bread on top. Press the sandwiches together and cut to shape. A nice variation is to use one slice of brown bread and one of white. Arrange the sandwiches on a serving plate and garnish with marigold petals and nasturtium flowers. Serve straight away.

STORECUPBOARD ESSENTIALS

*Both gardeners and cooks have always endeavoured to lengthen the life of the
herb garden beyond the summer. Unless you live in a climate where
your herbs will grow well all year round you will doubtless be keen to investigate
many of the traditional ways of preserving herbs.
The suitable methods extend from drying bunches of midsummer herbs to making
an aromatic purée or a well-flavoured preserve like a herb jelly.
Drying: this is one of the simplest techniques for preserving herbs
and is particularly suitable for the highly scented Mediterranean herbs such as
thyme, rosemary and lavender. The level of essential oils
secreted in the leaves of all herbs is highest just before the plant blooms.
Choose a dry day and pick the herbs in mid-morning before the heat of the sun
makes the leaves limp. Discard any old, tough or discoloured leaves
and strip the lower end of each stalk so that the bunch can be tied together with string.
Hang up in a warm place, preferably away from bright sunlight,
and leave undisturbed until the herb feels paper dry – the drying time depends
upon the level of humidity and the ambient temperature.
Next strip the leaves from the stalks and store in a screwtop jar in a dark cupboard.
The flavour of the dried herbs will be stronger if you store the leaves unbroken.
It's a simple matter of crushing or pounding them to a powder when required.
Herb jellies, sugars and syrups (see pages 79 and 89) are a delight to prepare.
These unusual preserves are indispensable for use in sweet dishes and desserts and the
high quality that you can achieve at home is virtually unobtainable commercially.*

PREVIOUS PAGE *left to right, front row* ROSEMARY JELLY, *page* 79; PEACH AND SWEET CICELY CONSERVE, *page* 79;

SAGE JELLY, *page* 79; KUMQUAT AND ANGELICA MARMALADE, *page* 79;

back row FENNEL VINEGAR, *page* 79; ROSEMARY OIL, *page* 86;

THYME OIL, *page* 86; DILL AND GREEN PEPPERCORN VINEGAR, *page* 79.

HERB VINEGARS

Almost all culinary herbs can be used to make a herb flavoured vinegar. The method could not be simpler: take a bottle of white wine vinegar and pour a little into a cup. Add your chosen herb to the bottle, for instance a long sprig of tarragon or a handful of leaves of basil. Pour back the reserved vinegar and seal the bottle tightly. Place the bottle in a warm room and leave for 1–2 weeks or until the vinegar has absorbed the aromatic oil from the herb. Use the herb vinegar as required, but store in a cool, dark place to preserve its flavour.

The principal herbs used for making herb vinegars are basil, bay, chervil, chives, dill, elderflower, fennel, garlic, juniper, lavender, lovage, marjoram, mint, nasturtium flowers, oregano, rosemary, sage, salad burnet, smallage, savory, tarragon and thyme. It is also worth making a herb vinegar by adding several herbs together. For instance, for a Provençal vinegar, add 1–2 cloves of garlic with a sprig each of thyme and rosemary to a bottle of white wine vinegar. In this way the cook can make a range of individual herb vinegars that are an asset in the kitchen.

PEACH AND SWEET CICELY CONSERVE

By adding just a sprig or a few leaves of the right herb you can transform the flavour of a jam, jelly or conserve into something quite exotic. Simply slide the herb into the hot jar of preserve before you seal and label it.

MAKES ABOUT 1kg (2¼lb)
1kg (2¼lb) ripe peaches
450kg (1lb) sugar
2 lemons
1 tablespoon peach brandy (optional)
4–6 sweet cicely leaves

Cover the peaches, 2–3 at a time, with boiling water, then lift out and remove the skins. Slice the fruit into a pan and discard the stones. (If you wish, you can crack a few stones and add the blanched kernels, sliced, to the peaches.)

Add the sugar and lemon juice to the peaches and place over low heat, stirring now and again until the sugar is dissolved. Then bring to the boil and boil until the conserve reaches setting point at 105°C (220°F). Remove from the heat. If desired, add the peach brandy to the conserve.

Place a sweet cicely leaf in the bottom of each of 3–4 small hot dry jars, spoon in the conserve, seal and label.
Note: this conserve does not set firmly. It is ideal for spooning over ice creams or on to a cream-topped scone.

KUMQUAT AND ANGELICA MARMALADE

Small orange kumquats, sliced into circles, make a fine-flavoured marmalade with the added interest of chopped angelica leaves which act as a 'sweetener' to the sharp citrus taste of the fruit.

MAKES ABOUT 1.8kg (4lb)
1kg (2¼lb) kumquats
600ml (1 pint) water
1–1.25kg (2–2½lb) sugar
1–2 fresh angelica leaves, chopped or 15g (½oz) candied angelica (see page 89), diced

Wash and dry the kumquats. Use a sharp knife to cut each kumquat into thin slices. Remove the pips and place them in a muslin bag. Place the fruit in a pan with the water and bag of pips. Bring to the boil, then simmer for 30–40 minutes or until the peel is tender.

Measure the contents of the pan and add 450g (1lb) of sugar for every 600ml (1 pint) of fruit pulp. Stir over low heat until all of the sugar is dissolved, then raise the heat and boil the mixture until setting temperature of 105°C (220°F) is reached, squeezing the pip bag occasionally.

Remove from the heat and discard the bag of pips. Stir in the fresh angelica leaves or the candied angelica and carefully pour the marmalade into hot, dry jars. Cover straight away or when cold.

HERB JELLIES

Herb jellies are one of the glories of the English store cupboard. A small pot of crystal-clear rosemary jelly is a wonderful partner to roast lamb or cold ham. Or a jar of claret and sage jelly makes an excellent accompaniment to roast pheasant or guinea fowl. The autumn is usually the best time of year to make herb jellies, when there are plenty of windfall apples around.

MAKES ABOUT 450g (1lb)
1–1.8kg (2¼–4lb) apples, washed and quartered
preserving or granulated sugar, warmed
juice of 1 lemon
fresh herbs: rosemary, thyme, chives, mint, marjoram, sage
green vegetable food colouring (optional)

Place the apples in a large pan with cold water to cover. Slowly bring to the boil, and then turn down the heat and allow to simmer for about 1 hour. Gently mash the fruit once or twice during the cooking.

Remove from the heat and cool slightly, then pour the contents of the pan into a jelly cloth or bag suspended above a bowl to catch the drips. Leave for several hours, preferably overnight, until all the juice has dripped through. It is important that you are not tempted to squeeze the bag or the final jelly will be cloudy.

Measure the juice into the clean pan and bring to the boil. For every 600ml (1 pint) of juice add 450g (1lb) of warmed sugar and stir over medium heat until dissolved. Boil until the jelly reaches setting point at 105°C (220°F). Add the lemon juice to the jelly and remove the pan from the heat.

If you wish, you can tint the jelly a pale green with just a drop or two of vegetable food colouring. Fill several small, hot dry jars with the jelly and add the appropriate herbs to each jar. Seal and label the jars.
Claret and sage jelly: replace one third of the strained apple juice with claret and proceed as above; add 3–4 finely chopped sage leaves to each jar of jelly, seal and label.

Mint, a herb commonly used for flavouring lamb, is an essential adjunct to many freshly made drinks – alcoholic as well as non-alcoholic. Whether it is added to a glass of iced tea or placed decoratively in a jug of cool southern mint julep, it provides a strong, refreshing flavour.

ICED TEA
WITH MINT AND LEMON

A frosted glass of iced tea decorated with borage flowers and a sprig of mint is guaranteed to allay the most fearsome thirst on a hot summer's day.

SERVES 6
3 rounded teaspoons Darjeeling tea leaves
4 sprigs of mint
1 litre (1¾ pints) cold water
caster sugar to taste
slices of lemon
borage flowers
a few extra sprigs of mint
borage flower ice cubes, made by placing
a borage flower in each ice cube
compartment before freezing

Measure the tea into a jug, add the sprigs of mint and pour on the cold water. Stir well, then cover and chill for 4–6 hours.

Strain the tea into a chilled serving jug, stir in sugar to taste and garnish with slices of lemon, borage flowers and sprigs of mint. Serve the iced tea in glasses with some of the borage flower ice cubes.

APRICOTS
PRESERVED IN EAU-DE-VIE
WITH LEMON VERBENA

This method of preserving dried fruit works equally well with fresh or dried cherries, dried pears and muscatel raisins.

450g (1lb) ready-to-eat dried apricots
225g (8oz) white sugar
300ml (½ pint) cold water
3 sprigs of lemon verbena
300–425ml (½–¾ pint) eau-de-vie

Check the apricots and remove any stalks or leaves. Place in a litre (2 pint) preserving jar: the fruit should fill just over half the jar.

Dissolve the sugar in the water over low heat, then bring to the boil and simmer for 5 minutes. Tuck the lemon verbena into the preserving jar and pour on the hot sugar syrup. Add eau-de-vie to the rim of the jar, making sure that it covers the fruit. Cover tightly and leave in a cold, dark place for 4–8 weeks before serving.

SOUTHERN MINT JULEP

One of the great classic cooling drinks – at its best served out of doors as the sun goes down. The distinctive flavours of mint and whisky complement each other deliciously.

SERVES 2
2 tablespoons crushed ice
2 cubes of sugar
6 mint leaves, lightly crushed to release
their flavour
2 tots of whisky or more according to
taste
2 sprigs of mint

The easiest way to make the crushed ice is to place ice cubes in a plastic bag on a solid surface and crush with a rolling pin. Divide the crushed ice between 2 whisky glasses. Add the sugar and mint and pour in the whisky. Stir briskly and serve when the glass is frosted, with more ice if liked and garnished with a sprig of mint.

PINK ELDERFLOWER
CHAMPAGNE

Everyone enjoys this traditional English fizzy, yet non-alcoholic, drink. The best time to make elderflower champagne is when the elder tree produces its creamy heads of blossom in late May and June – in fact, in some parts of the country this drink is known as June champagne. In other areas, it is known as Frontignan due to its muscat flavour which resembles the Languedoc wine of the same name. Elderflower champagne should be stored in strong sparkling wine bottles in a cold place for at least 2–3 weeks before opening and drinking.

MAKES 6 × 75cl BOTTLES
3 heads of elderflower in full bloom
300ml (½ pint) blackcurrants, fresh or
thawed
2 tablespoons wine vinegar
680g (1½lb) white sugar
4.6 litres (8 pints) cold water
6 champagne or sparkling wine bottles
plus corks and wires

Cut the large stems from the heads of elderflower and put the blossom in a large bowl or bucket. Add the blackcurrants, the vinegar and the sugar. Pour in the cold water and stir well. Cover the bowl with a cloth and set aside for 24 hours, stirring the mixture from time to time to release the juice from the fruit.

Next day, strain the liquid into bottles, and cork and wire them securely. Store the bottles on their sides in a cool, dark place for 2–3 weeks. The wine is ready when the corks start to rise in the wires. Take care when opening the bottle to point the cork away from any objects or people.

Fresh herbs always impart flavour and decoration to homemade drinks. An ingenious way of using them decoratively is to place them inside an ice cube and drop several cubes into individual drinks. As the ice cube melts it gradually releases a delicate taste of herbs into the drink.

RASPBERRY AND HYSSOP SHRUB

A shrub is a fruit-based cordial similar to the sherbet of the Middle East. For drinking on a hot day, the concentrated syrup is nicest served in thin glasses, and is diluted with plain or carbonated mineral water and ice-cubes.

1kg (2lb 3oz) raspberries
3 sprigs of hyssop
340g (12oz) sugar
juice of 1 lemon
mineral water
ice cubes containing flowers and/or leaves
of hyssop

Slowly bring the raspberries almost to the boil, stirring until the fruit begins to give up its juice. Remove from the heat and strain the fruit juice through a fine nylon or muslin sieve, gently pressing the fruit with a wooden spoon to extract all the juice.

Return the fruit juice to the pan and add the hyssop, sugar and lemon juice. Stir over low heat until the sugar is dissolved. Pour the fruit syrup into a jug and chill until ready to serve.

Discard the sprigs of hyssop and serve the shrub in glasses, diluted with mineral water and chilled with hyssop ice cubes.

TEAS AND TISANES

Herbal teas, tisanes and infusions can be made in tremendous variety and have an equally wide range of properties: stimulating or soothing, invigorating or relaxing, they have always been known for their therapeutic and medicinal qualities. They also make a delightful drink simply to enjoy in place of ordinary tea. Take time with these drinks to discover the flavours and strengths you prefer.

Strictly speaking, all teas are herb teas. For the China or India tea familiar to the English tea and breakfast table is simply an infusion of the leaves of the plant, *Camellia sinensis*. Like other members of the camellia family, the tea plant can be grown quite easily in mild regions of the British Isles – though its small white flower is no rival for the beautiful hybrid camellia. In the case of green teas the young leaves of tea plants are hand-picked and dried straight away, whereas black teas are produced by slightly fermenting the leaves before they are dried and graded.

All teas, tisanes and infusions made with edible herbs are green teas; the herb leaves can be used fresh or dried, though the amount used is halved when the herb is dried. I personally prefer the extra aroma produced by fresh leaves; the usual allowance is 2–3 teaspoons fresh herb leaves to 0.6 litre (1 pint) of boiling water. The herb is placed in a warmed teapot and boiling water is poured on top. If your water is highly chlorinated, use a mild-tasting, still mineral water to obtain the true taste of the herb. Leave the tea to brew for 3–5 minutes then pour the liquid through a strainer straight into the cup or glass – though first place a spoon in the glass to prevent it cracking. Add a slice of lemon if you wish and, if a

ABOVE *Aficionados will probably have a favourite teapot as part of the ritual: mine is a glass one, which I find both pretty and practical for the purpose.*

RIGHT *Fresh or dried flowers, leaves, hips and seeds are all suitable for herbal teas, though fresh and dried herbs will give noticeably different nuances and intensities of flavour.*

sweetener is needed, stir in clear honey rather than sugar. Milk is not added to herb teas. For the purest flavour it is essential that the teapot is scrupulously clean. I rather like to use a glass teapot for herb teas – it is attractive, easy to clean, and also enables you to look at the colour of the liquid and gauge the strength of the brew more easily.

Traditionally herb teas and tisanes have also been prescribed for the treatment of particular complaints or infections. Some had especially charming names, such as the French *Tisane de Sept Fleurs*, which is prescribed for sleeplessness, or Oswego Tea – the favoured beverage of the Oswego tribe of North American Indians – which became popular throughout the country during the eighteenth century, in the aftermath of the Boston Tea Party.

These days, herb teas are increasingly served as a pleasant-tasting and refreshing alternative to conventional tea or coffee. Herb teas with digestive properties like lime-flower or *tilleul*, and peppermint or *menthe*, have been highly popular in France for generations. They are served after dinner in the evening when the caffeine in black coffee can keep you awake. Though, as with all herbs, it is important to respect the individual properties of each plant. Some herbs produce a surprisingly powerful tisane – the tea *yerba mate*, for example, produces a tea which contains more caffeine than coffee.

When you start to drink herb teas it's a good idea to sample those made with a single herb to discover each individual flavour. Then gradually experiment with two or more herbs in the same pot until you discover a blend of herbs that pleases you.

HERBS FOR TEAS AND TISANES

ANGELICA, *Angelica archangelica*: use the leaves alone or with a strip of lemon zest.

BASIL, *Ocimum basilicum*: use the leaves alone or add 2 to a pot of Assam tea. Basil and sage tea is also very good.

BERGAMOT, *Monarda fistulosa*: the fresh or dried flower heads are used to make a tisane known as Oswego tea. For a milder flavour try adding a few flower heads to a pot of green China tea.

BETONY, *Stachys officinalis*: the leaves make a delicious tea that has a similar flavour to China tea. The addition of a short strip of orange or lemon zest, a piece of cinnamon bark or a few cloves are recommended. Betony tea was popular in the time of Caesar Augustus.

CHAMOMILE, *Chamaemelum nobile*: the flowers produce a pleasant herb tea specially recommended for drinking before retiring.

CARAWAY, *Carum carvi*: the fresh leaves produce a mild-tasting tea, the dried seeds give a stronger version.

CATNIP, *Nepeta cataria*: both the leaves and the flowers are used.

ELDERFLOWER, *Sambucus nigra*: the fresh or dried flowers make a fragrant, mild tea.

FENNEL, *Foeniculum vulgare*: the leaves, flowers and seeds can be used to produce teas of varying strength.

FENUGREEK, *Trigonella foenum-graecum*: use the dried seeds. For a stronger flavour bruise them in a mortar before adding to a pot.

HAWTHORN LEAF, *Crataegus monogyna*: both fresh and dried leaves are used.

HIBISCUS, *Hibiscus syriacus*: use the fresh or dried flowers and add a bruised cardamom pod.

HOLLYHOCK, *Althea rosea*: fresh or dried leaves produce a reddish liquid with a good flavour.

HYSSOP, *Hyssopus officinalis*: best made with fresh leaves and a strip of orange zest.

LAVENDER, *Lavandula* x *intermedia* 'Vera': use fresh or dried leaves or flowers, sweetened if desired.

LEMON BALM, *Melissa officinalis*: a classic herb tea. Use fresh leaves and sweeten with honey.

LEMON VERBENA, *Aloysia triphylla citriodora*: use fresh or dried leaves or flowers. Try adding a sprig of lemon balm to a pot of China tea.

LIMEFLOWER, *Tilia cordata*: one of the best herb teas; use fresh or dried flowers.

MINT, *Mentha* species: all varieties of mint make very fine teas – they are widely drunk in Mediterranean countries – use fresh or dried leaves and serve with thinly sliced lime or lemon.

RASPBERRY LEAF, *Rubus idaeus*: use fresh leaves for the best flavour and serve with a little zest of orange.

ROSE, *Rosa* species: both fresh and dried hips or petals make a classic herb tea which is often popular with young people.

ROSEMARY, *Rosmarinus officinalis*: use fresh or dried leaves; one of the best herb teas.

SAGE, *Salvia officinalis*: use fresh or dried leaves; a highly regarded herb tea – England used to export the dried leaves to China. Use with caution; not at all during pregnancy.

THYME, *Thymus vulgaris*: use fresh or dried leaves, an excellent digestive tea.

TEA RECIPES

ROSE-SCENTED GERANIUM TEA

SERVES 3

2 teaspoons gunpowder tea
3 leaves rose geranium
3 cloves

Place the tea, leaves and cloves in a warmed pot and pour on the boiling water. Stir, allow to infuse for 4–5 minutes, then pour.

DILL TEA

This tisane is a good digestive.

SERVES 3

2 teaspoons fresh or 1 teaspoon dried dill
5 cardamom pods, crushed to split their skins
¼ teaspoon dried mint or 1 teaspoon grated fresh ginger
0.6l (1 pint) boiling water
½ lemon cut in thin slices

Place the dill, cardamom pods and mint or ginger in a teapot and pour on the boiling water. Allow to infuse for 5 minutes, then serve with a slice of lemon for each person.

ICED EARL GREY AND LEMON VERBENA TEA

SERVES 4–6

3 teaspooons Earl Grey tea
3 sprigs lemon verbena
1.2l (2 pints) boiling water
honey to sweeten (optional)
ice cubes made with mineral water and leaves of lemon verbena

Measure the tea and lemon verbena into a heatproof jug and pour on the boiling water. Stir and leave to infuse for 5 minutes then strain into another vessel and allow to cool. Sweeten to taste with honey, if desired, then cover and chill. Serve in stemmed glasses with ice cubes.

PUREE D'AIL

The best garlic for making this very good purée is 2–3 months old with fat, juicy cloves. Serve the purée, at room temperature, with grilled meat.

MAKES ABOUT 600ml (1 pint)
4 large heads of garlic or 450g (1lb) garlic
salt
300ml (½ pint) cold water
2 bay leaves
8 tablespoons fruity olive oil

Peel the cloves of garlic, cut each in half and, if necessary, remove the green growing shoot in the centre. Roughly chop the garlic. Cook, covered, in the salted water with the bay leaves for 8–12 minutes or until tender. Remove from the heat, discard the bay leaves and strain the garlic into a food processor, reserving the cooking liquor and adding it as necessary to make a smooth purée. Then mix in the oil.

Spoon the purée into an airtight lidded jar. Seal tightly, label and store in a cold place until it is needed.

GARLIC PRESERVED IN OLIVE OIL

Whole heads of the new season's garlic are highly delicious preserved in an aromatic olive oil for winter use.

4–6 heads of garlic
600ml (1 pint) olive oil, approximately
a sprig of thyme
a sprig of rosemary
a few bay leaves

Remove the outer papery layers from the garlic until the separate cloves are uncovered, but leave them intact. Brush a sheet of baking parchment or foil with olive oil and place in a roasting tin. Arrange the garlic on top, then wrap the paper or foil securely around to enclose it. Bake the garlic in a moderately hot oven (190°C, 375°F, gas mark 5) for 15–20 minutes or until the cloves are tender.

Transfer the heads of garlic to a wide-necked preserving jar, tuck in the herbs and pour in enough olive oil to cover. Fasten down the lid of the jar and store in a cold place for 1–2 months before using.

The cloves of garlic are superb added to soups and casseroles.

HERB OILS

The magical combination of an aromatic herb with a fine olive oil is as ancient as it is satisfying. A virgin olive oil scented with a handful of basil leaves or a sprig of rosemary transforms the humblest salad into a very special dish. Although herb-flavoured oils have been used cosmetically for centuries, their principal role is in the kitchen.

The method for making them is indeed simple and akin to that for a herb vinegar. Take a bottle of extra virgin olive oil and pour a little into a cup. (Other good vegetable oils like sunflower, safflower, grape seed and groundnut oil can be used as an alternative to olive oil.) Add the herb to the oil, allowing 2–3 sprigs or 1–2 tablespoons of leaves to 300ml (½ pint) oil, and pour in the reserved oil. Seal the bottle and keep in a moderately warm room for 1–2 weeks until the oil has absorbed the flavour of the herb. Then strain the flavoured oil into another bottle and keep in a cold place until required.

HERBS RECOMMENDED FOR FLAVOURING OILS: bay, basil, chervil, dill, fennel, garlic, juniper, lavender, lovage, marjoram, mint, parsley, rosemary, sage, savory and thyme.

BOUQUET GARNI

Making a bouquet garni of fresh herbs is one of the great pleasures of herb gardening. Picking a bay leaf, a sprig of parsley and another of thyme and then tying them neatly with fine string is a task that any cook welcomes. The essential contribution of a fresh bouquet garni to a dish is invaluable and no amount of alternative seasoning can replace the unique flavour of fresh herbs.

The classic bouquet garni of French cooking consists of 2 sprigs of parsley, 1 sprig of thyme and a bay leaf tied together with thread long enough for tying it to the handle of the pan in order that it can be easily removed at the end of the cooking.

Which herbs comprise your bouquet garni is a matter of personal preference. There are, however, some established combinations which work well when cooking particular ingredients:

FOR CHICKEN AND TURKEY: parsley, chives or leek, thyme and a little celery

FOR BEEF: bay, parsley, thyme, 2 cloves and possibly a little orange zest

FOR LAMB: parsley, lemon thyme, bay and celery

FOR PORK: parsley, bay, thyme and lemon zest

FOR VEAL: parsley, bay, marjoram, lemon zest and sage

FOR GAME: parsley, bay, rosemary and 2 juniper berries wrapped in layer of leek

FOR TOMATOES: parsley, bay and basil or tarragon or hyssop

FOR BROAD BEANS: parsley, chives and summer savory

FOR PEAS AND MANGETOUT: parsley, mint and chives

FOR ROOT VEGETABLES: parsley, bay, oregano and thyme

FOR POTATOES: parsley and bay

FROSTED FLOWERS

The English enthusiasm for frosted flowers with their pretty apppearance and sweet taste dates back to Elizabethan cooking and earlier. Most seventeenth-century cookbooks include a wide range of flower recipes for cowslips, roses, violets and calendulas or pot marigolds. Provided that the plants are free from pesticide sprays, edible flowers can be picked and eaten straight from the plant. Frosting is a simple and effective way of preventing an edible flower from wilting and also preserves the bloom for later use.

The flowers of most herbs taste delightful, with a delicate flavour of the herb itself. I recommend basil, bay, bergamot, borage, chamomile, chervil, chive, claytonia, dill, elderflower, fennel, hyssop, lavender, lemon balm, lemon verbena, lovage, marjoram, mint, pineapple sage, purslane, rocket, rosemary, sage, salad burnet, sorrel, sweet cicely, tarragon, tansy, thyme and woodruff.

The following garden plants also have edible flowers: alyssum, anchusa, begonia, carnation, chrysanthemum, clover, coleus, cornflower, cosmos, cowslip, dahlia, daisy, day-lily, forget-me-not, geranium or zonal pelargonium, gladioli, hawthorn blossom, hibiscus, hollyhock, honeysuckle, hop flower, jasmine, lilac, lime flower, mallow, marigold, mesembryanthemum, monarda, nasturtium, hearts-ease pansy, pink, rose, sedum, stock, tiger lily and violets.

egg white
caster sugar

Lightly whisk the egg white and brush gently on to both sides of each flower or petal. Dust the flower all over with caster sugar and shake gently to remove excess sugar, leaving a thin layer. Place the flower on baking parchment on a wire rack in a warm place and leave for 1–3 hours until completely dry.

Store frosted flowers in an air-tight plastic box, although they taste best as soon as they are dry and before their scent evaporates. Use frosted flowers for decorating sorbets, ice-creams, cakes, custards and tartlets.

CANDIED ANGELICA

To make candied angelica, select some narrow tender stems and cut into 7.5cm (3in) lengths. Cook in boiling water until tender. Drain well and remove any tough outer skin, though with young angelica this is not usually necessary.

Weigh the angelica and layer it in a dish with an equal weight of caster sugar. Set aside for 1–2 days until the sugar has liquified. Transfer to a pan and heat gently until the liquid has almost evaporated. Place the pieces of angelica on a wire rack over a plate and leave in a warm place or a low oven for 1–2 days until dry. Store the candied angelica in an air-tight container and use as required.

These dishes of French herbs mixed into dried beans serve two purposes: not only are they decorative and aromatic, but they could also be kept in an airtight jar, placed in the storecupboard and used as a base for making delicious winter-warming soups. Good combinations to try would be chick peas and bay leaves, butter beans and sage or lentils and thyme.

HERB SUGARS

It is most fortunate for the pastry cook that the highly aromatic oil secreted by the leaves of a herb is readily absorbed by a jar of fine sugar. Scented rose petals make a delightful perfumed sugar that is perfect for sprinkling on custards, sponge cakes and biscuits.

Herbs recommended for perfuming sugar include angelica, aniseed, bay, rose geranium and other scented leaf geraniums, hyssop, lavender, lemon balm, lemon verbena, marigold flowers, mint – especially eau-de-cologne and pineapple mint, rose petals, rosemary, sweet cicely and sweet violet.

FOR LAVENDER SUGAR: layer 225g (8oz) of caster sugar with 60g (2oz) spikes of fresh lavender flowers or 30g (1oz) dried lavender flowers in a lidded jar. Leave in a warm place for 1–2 weeks, giving the jar a shake now and again to distribute the scent evenly. When the sugar has absorbed the scent of the lavender, sift the sugar to remove the lavender flowers. Keep the jar tightly sealed and use the lavender sugar as required.

Rose petal sugar is made in the same way. Select dry, highly-scented rose petals and arrange them in layers with caster sugar in a lidded jar. Leave in a warm room for 1–2 weeks and use the sugar as required by shaking it through a sieve to remove the rose petals.

HERB SYRUPS

A herb syrup is a most appealing way of capturing the scent of a herb for use later in the year. Herb syrups are an excellent way of sweetening and flavouring desserts like sorbets, ice creams and custards. Alternatively, a herb syrup can be used hot or cold as a sauce for a steamed pudding or an ice cream: for example, try drizzling a lemon verbena wine syrup over a freshly baked sponge cake just before serving with pouring cream.

The best herbs to use for making a flavoured syrup have a fairly strong scent: they include angelica, aniseed, elderflower, fennel, rose geranium and scented leaf geraniums, hyssop, lavender, lemon balm, lemon verbena, all mints, pineapple sage, rose petals, rosemary, sweet cicely and sweet violet.

Prepare a sugar syrup by dissolving 120g (4oz) caster sugar in 150ml ($\frac{1}{4}$ pint) water over low heat. Bring to the boil and simmer for 3 minutes, then remove from the heat and pour the syrup into a jar. Add 2–3 sprigs of the desired herb. Cover the jar and allow to cool. Discard the herb and use the syrup as required. Herb syrups store in a refrigerator for 2 weeks, or in a freezer for 2 months.

Herb-scented wine syrup is made by replacing half the water in a syrup with a medium dry or sweet white wine.

CULTIVATION CHART

HERB	FAMILY	TYPE	SIZE	SITE	SOIL	SUITABILITY
Angelica, *Angelica archangelica*	*Umbelliferae*	Biennial	1–2m	Light shade	Rich, damp	Specimen, back border
Aniseed, *Pimpinella anisum*	*Umbelliferae*	Half-hardy annual	40cm	Full sun	Rich, well-drained	Mid border
Basil, *Ocimum basilicum*	*Labiatae*	Tender annual	20–45cm	Full sun	Rich, damp	Front-mid border
Bay, *Laurus nobilis*	*Lauraceae*	Semi-hardy evergreen	up to 8m	Sun, light shade	Rich, well-drained	Specimen tree
Bergamot, *Monarda didyma*	*Labiatae*	Hardy perennial	up to 1m	Full sun	Rich, well-drained	Mid border
Betony, *Stachys officinalis*	*Labiatae*	Hardy perennial	4.5–6cm	Light shade	Rich, well-drained	Mid border
Borage, *Borago officinalis*	*Boraginaceae*	Hardy annual	45–75cm	Sun, light shade	Rich, well-drained	Mid-back border
Caraway, *Carum carvi*	*Umbelliferae*	Biennial	25–45cm	Full sun	Rich, damp	Front-mid border
Catmint, *Nepeta cataria*	*Labiatae*	Hardy perennial	0.5–1m	Full sun	Well-drained poor	Edge, front-mid border
Chamomile, *Chamaemelum nobile*	*Compositae*	Hardy evergreen	20–30cm	Full sun	Light, well-drained	Edge, paths, lawn
Chervil, *Anthriscus cerefolium*	*Umbelliferae*	Hardy annual	20–30cm	Light shade	Loamy, well-drained	Front-mid border
Chives, *Allium schoenoprasum*	*Liliaceae*	Hardy perennial	15–75cm	Sun, light shade	Rich, well-drained	Edge-front border
Clary, *Salvia horminum*	*Labiatae*	Hardy annual	30–45cm	Full sun	Moderately rich	Front-mid border
Claytonia, *Claytonia perfoliata*	*Portulacaceae*	Hardy annual	15cm	Light shade	Rich, damp	Front border
Comfrey, *Symphytum officinale*	*Boraginaceae*	Hardy perennial	1m	Sun, light shade	Rich, well-drained	Mid-back border
Coriander, *Coriandrum sativum*	*Umbelliferae*	Half-hardy annual	30–45cm	Full sun	Rich, light	Front-mid border
Cornflower, *Centaurea cyanus*	*Compositae*	Hardy annual	60–90cm	Full sun	Medium, well-drained	Mid-border
Curry plant, *Helichrysum italicum*	*Compositae*	Half-hardy evergreen	45cm	Full sun	Poor, well-drained	Low hedge, front-mid border
Dill, *Anethum graveolens*	*Umbelliferae*	Hardy annual	45–90cm	Full sun	Rich, well-drained	Front-mid border
Elder, *Sambucus nigra*	*Caprifoliaceae*	Deciduous shrub	3–5m	Sun, light shade	Moderately rich, damp	Specimen tree
Fennel, *Foeniculum vulgare*	*Umbelliferae*	Hardy herbaceous perennial	2m	Sun	Poor, light	Back border
Fenugreek, *Trigonella foenum-graecum*	*Leguminosae*	Tender annual	30–60cm	Sun	Rich, well-drained	Mid border
Feverfew, *Tanacetum parthenium*	*Compositae*	Hardy perennial	45–60cm	Full sun	Medium, light	Mid border
Garlic, *Allium sativum*	*Liliaceae*	Hardy perennial	30–45cm	Full sun	Medium, well-drained	Front-mid border
Geranium, *Pelargonium* species	*Geraniaceae*	Tender evergreen perennial	30cm–1m	Sun, light shade	Medium, gritty	Container, mid border
Hop, *Humulus lupulus*	*Cannabidaceae*	Hardy deciduous perennial climber	up to 7m	Full sun	Rich, deep	On a wall or support
Horseradish, *Armoracia rusticana*	*Cruciferae*	Hardy perennial	45–60cm	Light shade	Rich, damp	Mid-back, separate border
Hyssop, *Hyssopus officinalis*	*Labiatae*	Hardy evergreen perennial	30–60cm	Full sun	Medium, light	Low hedge, front border
Jasmine, *Jasminum officinale*	*Oleaceae*	Hardy, deciduous climber	up to 6m	Sun, light shade	Rich, deep	On a wall or support
Juniper, *Juniperus communis*	*Cupressaceae*	Hardy evergreen shrub	1–3m	Full sun	Well-drained, alkaline	Specimen, hedge
Lavender, *Lavandula angustifolia*	*Labiatae*	Hardy evergreen perennial	30–75cm	Full sun	Poor, light	Low hedge or edging
Lemon balm, *Melissa officinalis*	*Labiatae*	Hardy herbaceous perennial	1m	Sun, light shade	Poor, damp	Mid border
Lemon verbena, *Aloysia triphylla*	*Verbenaceae*	Half-hardy perennial	50cm	Full sun, sheltered	Poor, light	Front border
Lime, *Tilia cordata*	*Tiliaceae*	Deciduous perennial	10m	Sun, light shade	Deep, damp	Specimen
Lovage, *Levisticum officinale*	*Umbelliferae*	Hardy herbaceous perennial	2m	Sun, light shade	Rich, damp	Mid-back border
Marigold, *Calendula officinalis*	*Compositae*	Hardy annual	30–50cm	Full sun	Rich, damp	Front

HERB	FAMILY	TYPE	SIZE	SITE	SOIL	SUITABILITY
Marjoram, *Origanum* species	*Labiatae*	Hardy herbaceous perennial	15–30cm	Full sun	Poor, light	Edge, front border
Mint, *Mentha* species	*Labiatae*	Hardy herbaceous perennial	1cm–1m	Sun, light shade	Rich, damp	Separate border
Musk mallow, *Malva moschata*	*Malvaceae*	Semi-evergreen perennial	60cm–1m	Full sun	Poor, well-drained	Back border
Myrtle, *Myrtus communis*	*Myrtaceae*	Half-hardy evergreen perennial	2–3m	Full sun	Rich, well-drained	Container, specimen
Nasturtium, *Tropaeolum majus*	*Tropaeolaceae*	Hardy annual	15–30cm	Full sun	Poor, well-drained	Front border
Parsley, *Petroselinum crispum*	*Umbelliferae*	Hardy biennial	25–45cm	Sun, light shade	Rich, damp	Edge, front border
Pineapple sage, *Salvia rutilans*	*Labiatae*	Half-hardy annual	30cm	Sun, light shade	Rich, damp	Front border
Purslane, *Portulaca oleracea*	*Portulacaceae*	Half-hardy annual	15cm	Sun, light shade	Rich, damp	Front border
Rocket, *Eruca vesicaria sativa*	*Cruciferae*	Half-hardy annual	60cm	Sun, light shade	Rich, damp	Mid border
Rose, *Rosa* species	*Rosaceae*	Hardy deciduous perennial	up to 2m	Full sun	Medium, well-drained	Specimen, middle-back border
Rosemary, *Rosmarinus officinalis*	*Labiatae*	Hardy evergreen shrub	30cm–2m	Sun, sheltered	Light, alkaline	Hedge, specimen, back border
Rue, *Ruta graveolens*	*Rutaceae*	Hardy evergreen perennial	30–60cm	Full sun	Poor, light	Edge, container, front border
Sage, *Salvia officinalis*	*Labiatae*	Hardy evergreen perennial	30–75cm	Full sun	Medium, well-drained	Hedge, mid border
Clary sage, *Salvia sclarea*	*Labiatae*	Hardy biennial	up to 1m	Full sun	Poor, light	Mid-back border
Salad burnet, *Sanguisorba minor*	*Rosaceae*	Hardy herbaceous perennial	10–40cm	Sun, light shade	Poor, alkaline	Front-mid border
Santolina, *Santolina chamaecyparissus*	*Compositae*	Hardy evergreen perennial	20–45cm	Full sun	Poor, light	Edge, front border
Smallage, *Apium graveolens*	*Umbelliferae*	Hardy herbaceous perennial	30cm	Light shade	Rich, damp	Mid-border
Sorrel, *Rumex acetosa*	*Polygonaceae*	Half-hardy perennial	25cm	Light shade	Rich, damp	Front-mid border
Southernwood, *Artemisia abrotanum*	*Compositae*	Hardy semi-evergreen	60cm–1m	Full sun	Medium, well-drained	Hedge, mid border
Summer savory, *Satureja hortensis*	*Labiatae*	Hardy annual	15cm	Full sun	Rich, damp	Edge, front
Sweet cicely, *Myrrhis odorata*	*Umbelliferae*	Hardy herbaceous perennial	60cm	Sun, light shade	Rich, damp	Mid border
Sweet violet, *Viola odorata*	*Violaceae*	Hardy deciduous perennial	10–15cm	Light shade	Rich, damp	Front border
Sweet woodruff, *Galium odoratum*	*Rubiaceae*	Hardy perennial	30cm	Light shade	Rich, deep	Front-mid border
Tansy, *Tanacetum vulgare*	*Compositae*	Hardy herbaceous perennial	up to 1.25m	Sun, light shade	Medium, light	Mid border
Tarragon, *Artemisia dracunculus*	*Compositae*	Half-hardy perennial	30–60cm	Full sun	Rich, well-drained	Mid border
Thyme, *Thymus* species	*Labiatae*	Hardy evergreen perennial	2–30cm	Full sun	Well-drained, alkaline	Edge, front border
Wall germander, *Teucrium chamaedrys*	*Labiatae*	Hardy evergreen perennial	10–20cm	Full sun	Medium, well-drained	Edge, front border
Wild strawberry, *Fragaria vesca*	*Rosaceae*	Hardy evergreen perennial	15cm	Light shade, sheltered	Well-drained, peaty	Edge, front border
Winter savory, *Satureja montana*	*Labiatae*	Hardy evergreen perennial	30cm	Full sun	Well-drained, alkaline	Edge, front border
Wormwood, *Artemisia absinthium*	*Compositae*	Hardy, deciduous	60–90cm	Full sun	Light, well-drained	Mid-border
Valerian, *Valeriana officinalis*	*Valerianaceae*	Hardy herbaceous perennial	60cm–1.5m	Full sun	Poor, well-drained	Wall, mid border

INDEX

HERB SUPPLIERS AND NURSERIES

CHILTERN HERBS,
Bortree Stile,
Ulverston, Cumbria LA12 7PB

CORNISH HERBS,
Trelow Cottage,
Mawgan-in-Meneage,
Cornwall

HERITAGE SEEDS,

Henry Doubleday Research Association,
Ryton Gardens,
Ryton on Dunsmore,
Coventry CV8 3LG

HOLLINGTON NURSERIES LTD,
Woolton Hill,
Newbury,
Berkshire RG15 9XT

NETHERFIELD HERBS,
37 Nether Street,
Rougham,
Suffolk IP30 9LW

ROBIN HERB GARDENS,
Spring Acre Farm,
Thorpe-in-Balne,
Doncaster,
South Yorkshire DN6 0DZ

SUFFOLK HERBS LTD,
Sawyers Farm,
Little Cornard,
Sudbury,
Suffolk CO10 0NY

THE SEED BANK,
Cowcombe Farm,
Gipsy Lane,
Chalford,
Gloucestershire GL6 8HP

ACKNOWLEDGMENTS

BIBLIOGRAPHY

A Book of Fruits and Flowers, introduction by C. Anne Wilson, reprint of 1653 edition by Prospect Books, 1984

Boulestin, X. Marcel and Hill, Jason, *Herbs, Salads and Seasonings*, William Heinemann, 1930

The Compleat Cook and *A Queen's Delight*, reprint of 1655 edition by Prospect Books, 1984

Couplan, Francois, *Mangez vos soucis!*, Editions Alternatives, 1983

Culpeper Nicholas, *Complete Herbal*, reprint of 1826 edition by Harvey Sales, 1981

Eales's, Mrs. Mary, *Receipts*, reprint of 1733 edition by Prospect Books, 1985

Evelyn, John, *Acetaria*, reprint of 1699 edition by Prospect Books, 1982

Gerarde, John, *The Herball*, reprint of 1636 edition by Bracken Books, 1985

Glasses, Hannah, *The Art of Cookery made Plain and Easy*, reprint of 1747 edition by Prospect Books, 1983

Grieve, Mrs M., *Culinary Herbs and Condiments*, William Heinemann, 1933

Heath, Ambrose, Faber and Faber, 1953

Holt, Geraldene, *French Country Kitchen*, Penguin, 1985, Simon & Schuster 1990

Japanese Herbs and their Uses, Brooklyn Botanic Record, 1968

Launert, Edmund, *Edible and Medicinal Plants of Britain and Northern Europe*, Hamlyn Publishing Group Limited, 1981

Lowenfeld Claire, Back Philippa, *The Complete Book of Herbs and Spices*, David and Charles, 1974

Plat, Sir Hugh, *Delights for Ladies*, reprint of 1609 edition by Crosby Lockwood and Son Ltd, 1948

AUTHOR'S ACKNOWLEDGMENTS

Years before I had agreed to write a book about herbs I was well aware of the daunting size of the subject and its considerable literature. No group of plants can have been better documented, or for longer. This book, though, makes no claims to be encyclopaedic; it is simply a personal view of the herbs I grow and the pleasure they give me.

While working on the book I have received much kindness and generosity from many gardeners, cooks and herbalists. The staff of both the Lindley Library and Wisley Gardens of the Royal Horticultural Society have been patient and helpful. I should particularly like to acknowledge the valuable assistance of several friends. They have photographed gardens, obtained books and recipes and even sent parcels of fresh herbs from as far as Australia, Cyprus, North America, France and Scotland. I thank them all most warmly: Myrtle and Dorinna Allen, Elizabeth Baker, Rosemary Barron, Anna Best, Claire Clifton, Colin Capon, Jeannette and Suzanne Doize, Lisa Kalaydjian, Efterpi Kyriacou, Patsy Guyer, Nevin Halici, Richard Hoskins, Laura Hudson, Allen Lacy, Janette Marshall, Sri Owen, Maro Pambou, Christalla Pantelides, Claudia Roden, Cherry Ripe, Lazaros Sparsis and Julie Toll. Finally my affection and gratitude goes to my husband and children who tirelessly collected information, seeds and plants.

PUBLISHER'S ACKNOWLEDGMENTS

The publisher would like to thank the following people for their help in preparing this book:
Michael and Denny Wickham, Clock House, Coleshill, Nr. Swindon, Wiltshire; Simon Hopkinson of Hollington Nurseries; Mr and Mrs A.J. Radcliffe, Essebourne Manor, Berkshire; Ragna Tischler Goddard; Hollington Herbs, Woolton Hill, Newbury, Berkshire; Mr and Mrs M. Hale; Jane Croswell-Jones of The Grange, Whatley Vineyard, Whatley, Frome, Somerset; Lynne Robinson; Richard Lowther; Lin and David Lobb, Hayford Hall.
Special thanks to the following people for providing props for special photography:
The Hop Shop, Castle Farm, Shoreham, Sevenoaks, Kent; Stitches & Daughters, 5–7 Tranquil Vale, Blackheath Village, London SE3; Gallery of Antique Costume & Textiles, 2 Church Street, London NW8; Tobias & The Angel, 68 White Hart Lane, Barnes, London SW13; The Shaker Shop, 25 Harcourt Street, London W1; Enigma (stand 22), Persiflage (stand 25), Chenil Galleries, 181–183 Kings Road, London SW3; Perfect Glass, 5 Park Walk, London SW10; Ashill Colour Studio, Clovers, Church Street, Alcombe, Minehead, Somerset.
And special thanks also to all those people in England and France who very kindly permitted photography to take place in their beautiful homes and gardens.

PICTURE ACKNOWLEDGMENTS

12 Mike Busselle; 14 left Christian Sarramon; 14 right Yves Duronsoy; 17 Alex Dufort/Impact Photos; 18 Barque/Jerrican; 22 Campagne, Campagne/J.C. Roudil; 27 left John Garrett/Insight Picture Library; 27 right Campagne, Campagne/J.L. Garcia; 30 Mike Busselle; 32 above S. & O. Mathews; 32 centre Barrie Smith; 32 below Mike Busselle; 35 right Mike Busselle; 36 Pictures Colour Library/Tim Clinch; 40 Mike Busselle; 42 Michelle Garrett/Insight Picture Library; 45 Jean-Pierre Godeaut; 46 left Denis Hughes-Gilbey; 46 centre La Maison de Marie Claire/Blochlaine/Saulnier); 50 John Heseltine; 52 Jean-Pierre Godeaut; 54 John Heseltine; 56 left Mike Busselle; 60 John Garrett/Insight Picture Library; 66 Martin Breese/Retrograph Archive; 72 below Karen Bussolini; 75 right Tessa Traeger; 78 Denis Hughes-Gilbey; 80 Martin Breese/Retrograph Archive; 81 left Yves Duronsoy; 84 right S. & O. Mathews; 84 Scala; 84 Mary Evans Picture Library; 85 Camera Press.

The following photographs were specially taken for Conran Octopus by Debbie Patterson: 1, 2–3, 5, 6–7, 8, 10–11, 15, 16, 19–21, 24–26, 28–29, 33, 34–35, 37–39, 43, 44, 46–49, 53, 55, 56–59, 62–64, 67, 68–69, 72 above, 73–75, 76–77, 81 right, 82–83, 84, 86, 89, 90–1.